LANGUAGE

Its Origin and its Relation to Thought

LANGUAGE

Its Origin and its Relation to Thought

by

F.R.H. ENGLEFIELD

Edited by G.A. Wells
and D.R. Oppenheimer

ELEK/PEMBERTON
London

First published in Great Britain in 1977
by Elek Books Ltd
54/58 Caledonian Road, London N1 9RN
for Pemberton Publishing Co Ltd

Copyright © A. D. Englefield 1977

ISBN 0 301 76101 9 (Hardback)
ISBN 0 301 76102 7 (Paperback)

Printed in Great Britain by
Unwin Brothers Limited
The Gresham Press, Old Woking, Surrey
A member of the Staples Printing Group

Contents

Foreword

Ronald Englefield was a very unusual man. His native endowment of intelligence was probably not much greater than that of the general run of eminent thinkers, but the use to which he put it was exceptional. He did not achieve, or even try to achieve, academic distinction. Shortly after acquiring a first-class degree in languages in Cambridge, he served as an infantry officer in the First World War. During this period he resolved to spend his life exploring the nature of human thinking and human behaviour, by means of positive knowledge and clear reasoning, and excluding mystical and unscientific theories with which the subject has always been bedevilled.

For the next thirty-odd years he led a double life. He taught modern languages (he was an outstandingly good teacher); the rest of his time, apart from his recreations—entomology, microscopy and music—he spent reading, writing and thinking. His range of study was wide and included psychology, philosophy, history, anthropology, mathematics, zoology, physiology—the list could be extended indefinitely. The same might be said of many compulsive readers with wide interests; but Englefield was no dilettante. Every book that was not utterly trivial received the full treatment, with notes on the contents, copious quotations, and even more copious comment and criticism. Here, he displayed another peculiar trait. When confronted with a piece of pretentious nonsense, where most of us would toss the book aside with an impatient shrug, Englefield would apply himself with ferocious concentration to exposing the rubbish for what it was, with detailed quotation and argument. (Chapter 13 of this book, where he criticizes recent writers on language, gives some indication of his ability carefully to analyse and criticize views which are very remote from his own[1].) As a result he was able to illustrate, with horrifying clarity, the dangers of empty thinking — that is, the use of language to convey ideas inadequately backed by concrete experience.

The outcome of all this labour was a long manuscript, covering the evolution of intelligent behaviour in animals, the nature of abstract ideas, the nature and origin of language, the relation between language and ideas, and between language and mathematics. The publication of a work of this scope, by an unknown author, presented obvious difficulties. The present volume represents the attempt of two of Englefield's admirers to extract from the larger work the portions relating to language and combine them into a coherent whole. The task was undertaken at a time when Englefield's creative energies were flagging (he died, at the age of eighty-four, in January 1975). It involved excisions and rearrangements, but little else. Some of the mortar is ours, but the bricks are his. The wider implications stressed in the original manuscript are not here forgotten, and are particularly evident in Chapters 11 and 12, which form the climax of the book in that they show how man, having acquired language, uses it to lead him into endless error.

The subject of the historical origins of language is at present rather unpopular among linguists; for all extant languages are highly complex and are at most a few thousand years old, whereas artifacts found with fossil man, which had clearly been made skilfully and to standard patterns, suggest that language existed as much as a million years ago (cf. Clarke & Piggott, p.41[2]). From these facts it is usual to infer that evidence concerning the origin of language is not available.

Admittedly, to attempt to trace all known languages to some primeval ancestor or ancestors would be as vain as to try to discover the original musical instrument, the ancestral bas-

---

1. The criticism of Chomsky in Chapter 13 has already appeared in the 1974 issue of the annual journal *Trivium* (published by the University of Wales Press), and we are grateful to the editors for permission to use it here.
2. Details of works mentioned in the text of this book in an abbreviated way (sometimes, as here, simply by naming the author) are given in the Bibliography at the end.

soon or the primeval lute. If such a thing were conceivable it
would only be possible with the aid of historical documents or
archaeological remains. And manifestly these do not exist.
But the question, How did people come to talk at all?, is a
legitimate biological question and admits of a theoretical
solution. We have to explain how from the primitive communication of a higher ape a gregarious and social animal
could develop by stages the purely conventional sound
language which is what we now understand by the word
'language'. Since animals other than man have a limited
power of communication, and all known human societies have
a fully developed conventional language, we can attempt to
fill the gap by means of a hypothesis. It has become customary
to dismiss all such hypotheses as pure speculation. But the one
Englefield proposes can to some extent be tested by experiment, as he shows in Chapter 6. Another indirect way of
confirming his hypothesis is that it serves to make intelligible a
number of practices which survive among primitive peoples.
He deals with this aspect of the question in Chapter 11.

Englefield's argument will throughout be found perfectly
intelligible, and the reader needs no specialist qualifications.
A key point in the argument is that the purely conventional
languages of today must have been preceded by some form of
self-explanatory gesture-language; for conventional signs
could only follow self-explanatory ones, and it is important to
show how the transitions could have occurred. The survival of
early forms of writing enables Englefield to illustrate this process of transition to some extent. But his main problem is to
explain how men could think of making arbitrary noises to
represent ideas, and then gradually add to their number until
other modes of communication became unnecessary. In brief,
his theory (stated in full in Chapter 9) is that, with use, self-
explanatory gestures became curtailed until they were no
longer self-explanatory; and that, once it was recognized that
purely arbitrary—i.e. not in any way self-explanatory—signs
could serve perfectly well for communication between members of the same group, it came to be realized that arbitrary
sounds were as good as any other arbitrary signs, and had
many advantages of their own. What was required to make
this vital step possible was 'insightful' behaviour—a kind of

behaviour which, although not peculiar to man, is much more highly developed in him than in any of his relatives. Köhler used the term to mean knowing and understanding what one is doing, instead of trying to solve a problem by mere random trial and error. In the case in question, what was necessary was realizing that the essential character of a sign is that its meaning must be understood by both parties to the communication and need have no kind of analogy to the idea to be conveyed.

Until recently, many biologists would have said that Englefield's point of departure—the invention of a language of gesture—would require an animal very much cleverer than an ape. The assumed intellectual gap underlying this objection has become much smaller (and the credibility of Englefield's theory has been much enhanced) since the demonstration, by the Gardners (1971) and others, that chimpanzees can be taught to use a conventional gesture-language.[3] Young chimpanzees readily learn to interpret and to execute symbolic gestures, and thereafter use these gestures in what can only be regarded as conversation. They make requests, ask questions ('What that?' is a typical question) and express emotions by means of conventional gestures. What is more, they are capable of a considerable degree of abstraction and generalization. (The gesture for 'open' is used for opening a door, a box, a bottle, or even for turning on a tap.) They invent new gestures ('bib' is indicated by drawing the outline of a bib on the chest) and compounds of previously learnt gestures ('water-bird' for duck, 'fruit drink' for melon); and use word-order, in a systematic way, to express differences of meaning.

At present, it seems that the important gap between ape and man lies not, as is usually supposed, in the intellectual sphere—that is, in the ability to remember, to plan ahead, to generalize and form abstract ideas—but in motor skill. Repeated attempts to educate chimpanzees in the use of spoken language have shown fairly clearly that the ape is incapable of the fine control and coordination of the vocal apparatus which are needed for speech. On the receptive side,

3.   A recent popular account of this work is Linden's *Apes, Men and Language*, Pelican books, 1976.

it can acquire great skill in the interpretation of complex conventional sounds. So, for that matter, can the sheep-dog. The difference in motor skill corresponds to a difference in manual dexterity. The ape can peel a banana, but cannot learn to play the violin. These considerations do not provide great comfort to those who cling to a belief in man's separation from the rest of the animal kingdom. It remains to be seen whether the conventional gesture-language can be perpetuated in a colony of chimpanzees, without human intervention.

Half the mystery of language is disposed of if we realize that a non-human primate can use communicative gestures. The other half is: how did man come to use his voice for communicative purposes? And Englefield shows how, from the kind of gestural behaviour within the capacity of the modern chimpanzees, this further development could have occurred in man. He shows, in particular, that the transition implies conscious invention. Writing in the eighteenth century, Condillac and Monboddo accepted the possibility that language could have been *invented*, but after Darwin it became usual to suppose that it must have *evolved*. This, of course, was a merely verbal 'explanation' of the origin of language. When the idea of biological evolution became popular, the word was applied, by analogy, to many instances of gradual development, so that one could speak of the 'evolution' of democratic government, or of musical styles. No one could seriously maintain that these instances of 'evolution' had anything to do with genetics, or with natural selection. The mystics and fundamentalists continued to rely largely on the extensive resources of the deity to account for the origin of language. Englefield shows clearly that a conventional oral language cannot be imagined as gradually growing up from a nucleus of onomatopoeic sounds, that a vocabulary large enough to be of any use could not have *happened* in this way, that there must, therefore, have been deliberate invention. For this reason the first chapter of this book includes a brief discussion of the nature of invention. It has often been supposed that the invention of so elaborate an instrument and its adoption by all the members of the community requires an intellectual capacity and a degree of co-operation which could only have been reached in a community already in possession of language. To answer this objection is one of Englefield's fundamental tasks. Language must have come into existence somewhere in the frontier region between ape and man, and Englefield insists that there can be no solution to this problem except in terms of an intelligible psychological theory applicable to them both.

The subject-matter of this book crosses the boundaries between a number of specialist fields, including linguistics, social anthropology, animal behaviour and psychology. Many scholars would regard this as a display of academic bad manners. Let them continue to do so. Meanwhile it is interesting to compare Englefield's approach and conclusions with those of Eric Lenneberg, whose recent book *The Biological Foundations of Language,* 1967, bravely sets out to cut the barbed wire between the 'specialities' of linguistics, psychology, neurology, developmental paediatrics and evolutionary theory. He starts with the question: From what source comes the power of speech? Setting aside answers of a mystical type, he summarizes the prevalent type of rational view as one 'based on the principles of discovery and rational utilization of inarticulate sounds', with natural selection favouring the survival of individuals capable of putting successive discoveries to good use. This view, which is not far from Englefield's, Lenneberg flatly rejects, and he sets out to show that 'reason, discovery and intelligence are concepts as irrelevant for an explanation of the existence of language as for the existence of bird songs or the dance of bees'. If Lenneberg has succeeded in his object, it must appear that Englefield has failed in his.

In our opinion, it is Lenneberg who has failed. After giving a detailed critical survey of present knowledge of the anatomy and physiology of the organs of speech, of the cerebral structures concerned with language, of the development of speech in normal and retarded children, and of the nervous disorders causing derangement in the use of language, he devotes a chapter to the evolutionary and genetic problems. He concludes that nothing is known about how the talking animal evolved, except that the critical step had probably been taken before the diversification of human 'races'. In fact, he does not refute what he regards as the prevalent view; he simply abandons the attempt to answer the evolutionary problem.

A fact on which great stress has been placed by Lenneberg

and others, and which is supposed to demonstrate the uniqueness of man, is the functional asymmetry of the human brain, in which speech is normally controlled exclusively in the left cerebral hemisphere. This fact would be relevant to the origin of language only if it could be shown that this structural modification had come about *before* man began to talk. This seems very unlikely. Many animal genera possess peculiar faculties, served by peculiar anatomical structures; and in every case there is an evolutionary problem to be solved. For the present, it is reasonable to suppose that language was first used by a creature with a symmetrical brain. This creature was no doubt less fluent, and less reliant on language, than his garrulous descendants, just as the ancestors of the bat were less skilled at sonar-controlled flight than their modern progeny. The notion that structure and function develop progressively and simultaneously still seems to be the only alternative to a theory of divine intervention.

In a chapter headed 'Language and Cognition' Lenneberg mingles some interesting information with a great deal of portentous gobbledy-gook, all too typical of much recent theorizing about language. His main conclusion, translated into normal English, appears to be that in order to talk like a man one must think like a man. We cannot but agree. In his final chapter he discusses, in rather general terms, the specific peculiarities of *Homo sapiens* which make him, alone among animals, capable of acquiring and using a language. The essential, he seems to be saying, is a specifically human 'cognitive function', latent in infancy and maturing (along with the ability to learn to speak) in early childhood. The theory of language which he propounds is too obscurely expressed to be easily summarized, but it appears to aim at giving scientific respectability to the linguistic theories of Noam Chomsky.

Lenneberg throughout his book speaks of 'natural' languages, meaning languages which are or have been in ordinary use, as opposed to inventions such as Esperanto. In Englefield's terms, these languages are conventional, being based on what appear to be arbitrary associations between sounds and meanings, whereas in a 'natural' language there would be a manifest connexion between signs, of whatever kind, and meanings. The problem of how a 'conventional' language could develop from a 'natural' one is a major concern for Englefield, but is hardly mentioned by Lenneberg. Another difference between the two lies in the field of comparative psychology. Englefield is concerned with the formation of abstract ideas in man and other animals, and discusses the evidence in some detail. Lenneberg speaks in general terms of 'cognition' and 'modes of categorization' in animals, but does not attempt to explain the special features of human cognition. Still less does he justify his initial assertion that 'reason, discovery and intelligence' are irrelevant to the discussion (unless, that is, 'cognition' is regarded as something unrelated to reason). On the subject of invention and discovery, which is of prime importance in Englefield's work, Lenneberg says nothing.

The foregoing remarks should not be construed as a general attack on Lenneberg. His is a good and valuable book, which would have been even better if he had made the extra effort to write in simple and intelligible prose, and if he had not strayed into the desert of Chomskyan metaphysics. We feel that he might have profited from reading Englefield's Chapter 12.

It may be observed that most of the books referred to in the text were written before 1940. This should not be taken to imply that the book is out-of-date. It is a common failing among academics to garnish their writings with references to the most recent publications, even if these are not strictly relevant to their arguments. Englefield did not have to defend his title to an academic post by this kind of display. It is really not surprising that the writings of two centuries before 1940 should contain more of relevance to the subject than those of the last quarter of a century. It can be seen from Chapter 13 that Englefield's reading did not stop at 1940. The large amount of work on psycho-linguistics which has been carried out in recent years, whatever may be its general interest and importance, has very little bearing on the questions with which Englefield was concerned. An exception is the work of the Gardners referred to above, on the acquisition of an artificial gesture-language by a young chimpanzee. This, and other recent works, are referred to in editors' footnotes.

One thing which Englefield found most lacking in modern writings on language was a clear view of the psychological processes involved in the formation and communication of ideas. To be acceptable these principles must be applicable, not only to man, but to his ape-like predecessors. It is here that Köhler's enormous contribution to the understanding of the thinking process in chimpanzees becomes so important. The mistaken idea that thinking depends on the use of words (or even *consists* in inner speech) dies hard. Englefield is at pains to show its falsity; further, he shows how misunderstanding of the nature of thinking, and of the real usefulness of words, has led to the proliferation of magical beliefs and of sterile philosophical theories, among other aberrations. He was convinced that when we understand the *normal* process of thinking and of expressing our thoughts, we shall have a better chance of seeing what leads to such misapplications of language. His arguments concerning the relation of words to ideas and to things form a substantial part of his contribution. The question of the origin of language is a matter of theoretical interest, but this other question — the relation between language and reality, and the insecure connexion between words and ideas — is of fundamental practical importance.

In tackling all these matters, Englefield has reminded us of a number of unjustly neglected writers of the past. Today, the portentous utterances of Schlegel, Humboldt and their like are quoted with respect, whereas the lucid commonsense of Condillac and Monboddo is largely disregarded. It is our hope that Englefield's writings will not share the neglect suffered by his eighteenth-century predecessors.

G. A. WELLS
Birkbeck College, London
D. R. OPPENHEIMER
Trinity College, Oxford

Preface to introduce Dinah and Sarah

Numerous references will be found in the course of this book to Dinah and Sarah, and in case the reader may wish to have some further information about them I will here formally introduce them. Dinah is a black Labrador dog about twelve years old, and Sarah is her daughter, some four years younger. They are the constant companions of the author who has not neglected the many opportunities they have given him of observing their ways, studying their language and divining their thoughts. Of their private characters it would be indiscreet to speak here; but this I may say, that although neither is free from that original sin to which we are all heirs, yet each of them has virtues which would adorn any mortal, no matter of what race or species.

CHAPTER 1

Ideas and Invention in Man and Other Mammals

The points of resemblance between men and other animals are many and obvious. They are also, on occasion, embarrassing, and there have been many attempts to find reassurance by insisting on some essential difference which sets man apart from all other species. It is the possession of language that has most often been regarded as the unbridgeable gap between ourselves and our nearest relatives. Language, it is said, is quite different from other forms of behaviour. It is obviously not purely instinctive, but has to be learnt, like swimming or skating. But somehow it is different, unique, and above all mysterious. I wish to challenge the notion that language is more of a mystery than other human accomplishments, such as learning to draw, count, or ride a bicycle. All these activities, I shall argue, are comparable, and not different in kind from the learning of which other animals are capable.

Many recent writers have denied that human language can have been evolved from any system of animal communication because they suppose that 'evolved' in this context means evolved as the bat's wing or horse's hoof were. It is rightly regarded as ridiculous to suppose that human language has, in this sense, evolved. But it is erroneously held that the only reasonable alternative view is that human language is innate. The possibility that it could have been invented is overlooked or rejected. Human language is a collection of noises, produced by the voice, arbitrarily linked to ideas. In so far as other animals communicate by means of vocal noises, these are mainly instinctive reactions. Humans also exhibit instinctive vocal reactions, but human speech is composed of *arbitrary* sounds and is, I shall argue, the result of conscious invention. Man is, beyond dispute, the most inventive of animals. Cats, dogs and apes discover new ways of gaining their ends, and so exhibit rudimentary powers of invention; but the difference between human and animal communication is not greater than the difference between human invention in general and animal invention. The fact that men communicate by means of arbitrary sounds, whereas apes do not, is indeed a striking difference, but no more remarkable than the fact that apes do not make use of bows and arrows, clothes or agricultural implements.If we consider human communication to be, like these, an invention, we shall find it easier to understand than if we suppose it to have been evolved like a limb or wing, or produced by some mysterious human 'creative ability'.

If we are to understand human thought and inventive capacity, we must study the thinking process in other mammals. The behaviour of dogs and apes shows clearly enough that although they lack words, they have ideas — by which I mean some inner mental representation of the external world. Among the earliest, and the most illuminating, observations on this subject were those of Wolfgang Köhler, who spent the years 1913 to 1920 observing a colony of captive chimpanzees on the island of Tenerife. Köhler offered his chimpanzees a primary goal — food — which was not directly accessible but could be reached only with the aid of a tool, such as a stick or ladder. The finding and application of the tool thus became a secondary goal, and attaining it involved turning aside from the primary goal, so that the food was no longer visible. Success in the task necessarily involves the persistence in the animal's mind of the image, or idea, of the primary goal. The following example illustrates what is involved. Fruit was attached to the roof and could be easily reached by standing on a box. The only available box, however, was out of sight in an adjacent corridor. Sultan, who seems to have been one of the geniuses of the little community of chimpanzees, was taken along the corridor before the experiment to make sure he knew the box was there. When the fruit was placed in position he made various attempts to reach it, and eventually exerted himself to detach a bolt from the door, apparently with the object of using it as a stick. While thus operating he hung on the door in such a position that he could not see the fruit. Nor could he see the box in the corridor. This is Köhler's account of what happened:

> Abruptly and without any external occasion, Sultan stops working at the bolt, remains for an instant motionless, then jumps to the ground, gallops along the corridor, and returns immediately with the box. (p.38)

In this case it is clear that, at the moment when Sultan stopped motionless, although both the primary and the secondary goals were invisible to him, they were nevertheless represented in his brain.[1] He obviously saw, in his mind's eye, the fruit, the box, and himself moving the box to under the fruit. We can explain his behaviour by supposing that he was able to carry in his mind an idea, or inner representation of the primary goal, and of himself achieving that goal with the aid of the secondary goal. In other words, he carried out, in imagination, a manipulation which he then proceeded to carry out in fact. It is in this power to form ideas and to manipulate them internally that we see the basis of human thoughts and human inventions. Thinking consists essentially of performing such experiments in the mind.[2] It consists in doing in the imagination what one has learnt to do with one's body. I can think of taking a walk with the dog because I have performed the actual operation. I do not need any words. A man who is used to working with his hands, to making things or manipulating them, will think in terms of such practical behaviour. The fact that Köhler's apes can do this too shows that, here again, words are not essential. When the kind of tool the ape requires to reach the goal is not available, he seeks substitutes. Thus, for a stick, are substituted branches torn from trees, metal bars broken from a shoe-scraper, screwed-up bundles of straw, and even an old shoe. These are not all equally effective but they are made to work. But sometimes a flexible plant stem, a single straw, or a strip of cloth are resorted to. Such substitutes have a certain appearance of suitability because of

1.   Vygotsky (p.39) states that the ape is incapable of doing just what Köhler shows that he *can* do, namely solve the problem when the tool is out of sight.
2.   This has been cogently argued by Mach and Rignano.

their form, but they are soon abandoned after, or even before trial. It is as if the ape had framed for himself a definition of the tool required, not of course in any kind of language, but in terms of the task to be accomplished. A certain length, a certain width (determined by comparison of visual aspects), a certain weight, a certain rigidity (determined by muscular and tactile aspects), provide a kind of specification in the brain, by reference to which each object that presents itself is judged appropriate or not.

In studying the behaviour of any animal we have to distinguish the *real* from the *sensory* situation—that is to say, the actual state of the animal's environment at any moment from the effect which it has on him through his sense organs and nervous system. It is the real situation on which his life depends, but it is the sensory situation which affects his behaviour. In the higher mammals the data of the senses are worked up—by a nervous process occurring in the brain—into a more and more faithful representation of the real situation. The primitive aquatic creatures that live in a rock pool (e.g. the Ciliates described by Jennings) know nothing of the shape, colour or distribution of the stones and weeds and other living creatures, but react merely to the chemical state or to the temperature of the watery medium in their immediate neighbourhood or to the vibrations or radiations (particularly the distribution of light and shadow) which happen to reach them.[3] To the fish the same pool is a world full of local features, with a sandy bottom for scavenging, a warm surface for basking, various cosy hiding places, and so on, and he knows how to find his way to any part of his familiar territory as his feelings prompt him. This involves reacting to specific objects, not merely to chemical and physical conditions in a medium. The terrestrial mammal has a far more complex knowledge of its environment, and becomes acquainted with many more features of the real world. Since an object presents different aspects when seen from different points of view, such an animal must be able to recognize its various projections as equivalent, and this requires an elaborate apparatus in the

---

3. Jennings, pp.48, 134; Fraenkel and Gunn, p. 136.

brain. The cry and the visible appearance of the cat may vary a good deal at different times and yet evoke the same response in the dog. Furthermore, the dog responds equally readily to the smell of the cat as to its cry or shape. The sound or smell or appearance seems to give rise in the mind of the dog to an *idea* of the cat, and the behaviour of the dog is determined by that idea. Köhler has demonstrated that the behaviour of chimpanzees is likewise intelligible only if one supposes that such ideas, or inner representations, take place.

Many students of animal behaviour will object to the introduction of psychological terms such as 'mind' and 'idea' into the discussion. Their use is justified, for the time being, by convenience. We may look forward to the day when the language of psychology is strictly translatable into the language of cerebral physiology: but that time has not come.[4] We still cannot describe our human neighbour's behaviour adequately without using the language of psychology; and the same is true of Köhler's descriptions of the behaviour of apes. Barnett (p.209) rightly insists that Köhler's ape was inventing when he substituted a plant stalk, a stone, and the other objects for the stick that he had been using to obtain food. It is possible to see how, out of the experimental beginnings suggested by chimpanzee behaviour, there developed an interest in the different uses of a thing, and hence in its various qualities; how the simple correction of an imperfect tool grew into the fashioning of special implements out of the selected materials and in different designs; how the quest for particular articles and materials led to an interest in their sources, their origin and their history; and how significant situations became extended not only in space but in time, so that it became necessary to inquire into their antecedents in order to identify them.

Science has developed out of the observation of correlations between external things or events. As the situations to which man's behaviour was adapted became more extended and more complex, both in space and time, the elements which

---

4. Until we are able to give an intelligible account of behaviour in simple psychological terms, it is premature to attempt interpretations, as does Parry, by reference to mathematical theories about mechanical systems of communication.

attracted his attention became ever more removed from direct relation to his bodily actions and he became more and more able to take an interest in external events and their relations to one another, without connecting them with himself. His social conditions favoured this tendency, for in watching the behaviour of his fellows he was in fact observing such external relations, even though one element in the relationship was a man like himself. That this was one way in which he could be introduced to an objective view of things is suggested by the interest which chimpanzees, according to Köhler, may occasionally show in one another's performances (cf. also below, p. 18).

At the earliest stage of human invention there could be only the use of implements supplied by nature, and invention consisted, as in the case of the ape, in learning new ways of using them. New methods could be discovered only by accident or experiment, but in man the more developed brain with its resources of stored experience would shorten many processes and make others possible. In man external and bodily experimentation is supplemented and partly replaced by internal or imaginary experimentation, i.e. thought or reflexion. In this internal trial-and-error behaviour, memories of the acts and their effects take the place of the actions and experiences which constitute external trial-and-error behaviour. Reasoning is the internal experiment, the experiment not with sticks and stones, but with the ideas of sticks and stones (cf. above, p. 3). But internal trial and error can only use the materials previously provided. A man cannot design an umbrella if he has never had any experience of rain. In addition to the material means there must also be an idea of the nature of the need.

External experiment may lead to new conjunctions and it will check and sometimes correct the false constructions of the mind; but it can never carry an animal very far beyond his customary range of achievement. By external experiment we may discover a new recipe for jam, but not a scheme for irrigating a desert. Our language suggests an illusory simplicity. We speak of looms and weaving as we speak of knives and cutting. But while chance may put a broken flint into a man's hand if only he has the habit of picking up small objects, chance will not set up a loom for him. Nevertheless every element or ingredient with which the imagination works has been derived from some direct sensory experience gained in commerce with the concrete world. Experiment is the only process we can understand by which an animal can get to know his world. It begins with the blind groping of the proto-zoon which probes its world by tentative excursions. Such mechanical exploration is elaborated by the development of new sense organs but does not at first reach far into sur-rounding space, and scarcely at all into time. Eyes and ears and nose extend the range of passive experience but not the range of physical experiment. But the memory stores, and the imagination experimentally rearranges, the successive patterns of experience, thus making possible those composite and far-ranging explorations which yield human knowledge. Yet the mind can only direct and suggest; its experiments, though unlimited in scope, are made with uncertain materials and its constructions must always be realized in concrete form before they can be tested.

The ape's power of making internal experiments—i.e. experiments in the imagination—is very limited. Again, animals can rarely transmit their discoveries; each individual learns from his own experiments but not from those of his fellows, so that every generation must start again from scratch. On the other hand man has the advantage over the other animals in just these two respects. His much increased capacity for carrying out experiments in the imagination may greatly abridge the period of trial leading to discovery, and often sug-gests fruitful combinations which could never arise by a lucky chance. And in the second place his ability to communicate ideas allows him to take over knowledge, methods and even ready-made tools from his companions, so that each gener-ation is in a position to progress a little further than its pre-decessor.

These advantages are offset by an increased liability to error. Experimenting in the imagination is unreliable, and in cases where the results cannot be checked by practical exper-ience often leads to fantastic errors. Similarly the attempt to transmit ideas through the medium of language, whenever verbal description cannot be illustrated by some kind of tangible demonstration, commonly results in the grossest distortion and degradation of those ideas. But it is fundamentally the same mental processes which in suitable circumstances produce effective behaviour, knowledge and science, and in other circumstances magic, myth and metaphysics.

The inventions of the ape are closely related to the immediate situation. But there is sometimes an interval during which the animal seems to have ceased to concern himself with the problem he cannot solve, and yet evidently carries in his mind some trace of the unresolved situation.[5] Now in man this interval may be longer. He can carry his problems about with him for indefinite periods, so that the terms of one may recur to him while he is engaged on the solution of another. When he is sawing or scraping he strikes fire. But this startling experience will lead to a discovery only if it finds, waiting for it in his mind, the necessary fructifying idea. Only the relation between the manual operation and the sparks in the wood shavings is supplied by the immediate experience, which is a chance by-product of another activity. The idea which fertilizes it may be the result of some recent special experience or the permanent residue of chronic worries, or it may be some unique experience recalled by luck at the right moment. The possibilities depend on the individual—not only on whether the necessary experiences are separately recorded in his mind, but also on whether it is capacious enough to allow all the relevant memories to come together at the same time. In such

5.   Sultan was on one occasion given two canes of about equal length, but of which one was slender enough to be inserted into the hollow end of the other. The goal was placed outside the bars and so far away that it could not be reached with a single cane. After some vain efforts with one stick Sultan let this stick fall outside the bars and used the other to push it towards the fruit. He succeeded in touching the fruit but not, of course, in drawing it in. After a while Köhler tried to help him by poking a finger into the hole at the end of the larger cane. Sultan seemed to pay no attention to this and retired to sit on a box not far away. Presently he got up, went and picked up both canes and returned to his box, where he sat down and began to play with them. While engaged in apparently aimless twiddling he chanced to bring the two ends together so that one cane fitted into the hole of the other. Immediately he darted forward to the bars—he had been sitting with his back half turned to them—and began to pull in a banana with the double stick. The sticks fell apart, but he at once put them together again and reached the goal.

cases the indispensability of internal trial and error is evident. The experiences which in collaboration give significance to the discovery cannot occur together except in the memory. We cannot suppose that a man, amusing himself with a lump of clay, happened to produce a cup-shaped object, happened to put it in the fire, happened to take it out again when it had been baked, and then happened to find it useful as a receptacle. But combinations of material circumstances that cannot be expected to occur spontaneously may nevertheless be imagined. Separate experiences and operations, too slow and arduous to be by luck combined in the concrete, may be combined in the imagination in all kinds of possible and impossible ways. The mind is an imaginary workshop and in times of quiet and leisure it is the scene of many novel experiments.

At first, then, nature provided the tools and weapons, and men had merely to learn to use them skilfully and select them with understanding. Next they learned to improve the rude products of nature. The process of elaborating the natural product grew ever more important until improvement became manufacture. Art, from being merely ameliorative, became creative. The contribution of nature, from being an unfinished article, became no more than a raw material. The thoughts of the inventor turned more to shapes and substances than to usable objects. The preparation of natural materials became more important than the utilization of natural objects. The products of nature, instead of being used as they were found, were broken up into their components, cooked, crushed, melted, moulded, until they yielded something still more useful. The composition or constitution of a thing became a matter of interest, and by becoming a constructor of things himself man became more curious concerning the structure of natural things. This transition from the first stage of invention, when nature was ransacked for usable objects, to the later stage when she was expected to furnish only plastic materials, resulted in one of the more conspicuous differences between human and animal invention.

The various forms of human communication cannot have been among the earliest inventions, for it must have been through co-operation in enterprises already involving the use of simple inventions that language was developed, as I shall try to explain later. Yet there can be little doubt that some forms of communication were early, and greatly influenced and accelerated the inventions which came after.

I turn now to a study of the conditions which led to the invention of language and shall try to show that they are essentially the same as those which underlie invention in general.

CHAPTER 2

The Origin of Communication

Most of the behaviour of an animal is closely related to its environment, which includes other animals. Some, at least, of its behaviour must be adapted to these and must therefore become highly specialized. Animals, being endowed with senses, are subject to influences which do not affect inanimate things. The latter must be subjected to physical pressure, whereas the former may be scared or excited or allured and in various ways *induced* to do things, without any apparent physical mediation. All the higher animals learn to influence the behaviour of other animals by playing on their senses. Sheep in a flock, for instance, are affected by the movements of the sheep-dog which they see and by his barking which they hear, and the dog controls their behaviour through their senses and brain without making contact with them.

The eyes, ears and nose were called by Sherrington 'distance receptors' because they enable an animal to become aware of distant conditions and events. On the same principle we may call the voice and motions of the animal, so far as they affect the behaviour of other animals without contact, *distance effectors*. The appropriateness of the expression with reference to the voice is fairly obvious. But the movement of the limbs, the attitude of the body, and the expression of the face, are equally capable of influencing other animals at a distance. The display postures of birds, and threatening gestures, which are found even among fishes, are as effective at a distance as warning cries or mating calls. In all such behaviour two parties are involved, the one which exerts the influence and the one which is subjected to it, and I shall refer to these as the *agent* and the *respondent* respectively. The same animal will, of course, play both parts at different times and even in rapid succession. Where the relation becomes mutual we have the rudiments of communication.

The psychological influence thus exerted by one animal on another is not necessarily deliberate. The scent of one may strongly affect the behaviour of another, though this behaviour is indifferent to the first, or even detrimental. Both action and response may be instinctive and, where such behaviour is adaptive, it may perhaps be called communication. But it has little relation to human communication which is derived from the intelligent behaviour of mammals. Perhaps it would be as well at this point, in view of the changing fashions in psychological terminology, to remind the reader that, as the words are here used, 'instinctive' differs from 'intelligent' behaviour in that the former tends to be uniform and stereotyped—i.e. all the individuals of a species act in the same way in the same situation—whereas the latter consists of acquired habits which, of course, vary according to the experience of each individual. Thus, if we wish to give a plausible explanation of the origin of human communication we must trace it to a non-stereotyped form of reaction capable of being gradually modified and elaborated under the guidance of experience.

Since types of behaviour can be evolved only out of pre-existing types, we have to show how communicative behaviour arose out of some non-communicative form. Evolution involves re-adaptation. New forms of behaviour do not arise out of nothing, any more than new organs. They can only be the result of the gradual modification of older ones. We have to conceive, therefore, a primitive type of human communication which could have emerged naturally out of some other kind of behaviour and which, at the same time, could by further modification give rise to language as we know it.

For convenience in the following discussion I shall distinguish *communicative* from *executive* acts. The former are intended to influence the behaviour of another man or animal, the latter to bring about any other kind of change in the environment. A man may remove his hat in order to mop his brow or to convey a greeting to a friend. In the former case the act is executive, in the latter communicative. Since all actions that are not communicative are executive, if deliberately performed, and since, by the principle of re-adaptation, all communicative acts must have been derived from non-communicative ones, our task can be simply expressed by saying that we must trace all communicative behaviour to executive.

In the development of communication the respondent is as important as the agent. No system of signs is of any use unless there is another animal that understands them. The importance of the respondent is shown in the relation between animals and men. Dogs have considerable powers of communication when dealing with human companions, much less in their dealings with one another, for the respondent needs not only senses to perceive but a brain to understand the signals. In the association of dog and man, it is the man who furnishes the chief stimulus, both as agent and respondent. In the one case he makes a variety of demands on the animal's powers, and in the other he responds helpfully even to the crudest signals, which are thus encouraged and differentiated. The development of communication is thus a reciprocating process in which agent and respondent provoke and inspire one another.

In order that the respondent may take an active part in the relationship, the things which he is induced to do must be of interest to him as well as to the agent. And it is only in social or co-operative behaviour that this condition can be fulfilled. Language can arise only in a social animal where there is real co-operation in common tasks, where each adjusts his behaviour not only to the nature of the task, but also to the behaviour of his companions. In an individualistic enterprise it is necessary only to cope with the material conditions; but in a co-operative enterprise the situation is continually being complicated by the presence of other workers who alter those conditions. In learning to take account of this additional factor it was necessary to develop the use of distance effectors.

Thus co-operation created the conditions for the development of language; yet it is also true that language facilitated co-operation, and alone made the specifically human forms of it possible. The two processes were really inseparable. But language in the highly conventional form that we know was by no means necessary. At the beginning co-operation and communication could hardly be differentiated. Every action by which a man shared in the common work might not only directly forward the work but also influence the other workers who could be thereby guided in the actions they themselves performed. And the action, according to its observed effects, could be adapted for either purpose. Interest in the other man's contribution would be increased by any want of harmony, interference or mutual obstruction, and attention would in such cases be drawn to the aims as well as to the consequence of his actions. Conditions would vary for each enterprise, but always there would be two learning processes involved: each man would gradually learn the effects of his own actions on others, and the significance of their actions for himself.

The first of these two learning processes may be described as follows. An action, normally performed for one purpose, is seen to produce a secondary effect which is as useful as or more useful than the primary effect. The action then comes to be performed specifically for the sake of the secondary effect, and is then gradually modified in adaptation to its new function. For instance, a man, by pushing or pulling, tries to shift an obstacle which hampers his movements. He does not shift it very much, but his action is noticed by a companion who, seeing his purpose, comes to his aid. The pushing was an executive act, but it happened to have a communicative effect. If this is observed by the pusher he may, on a future occasion, perform the action *in order* to elicit assistance—i.e. for the sake of its communicative effect. If so, the action may well become adapted to its new function by being curtailed into a mere gesture of pushing. Children may be seen to try, or to pretend to try, to do something obviously beyond their powers, in order to induce somebody to help them. Dogs too will sometimes make fruitless efforts to obtain some object with the apparent aim of attracting assistance. Thus the first important step towards deliberate communication is taken when a man initiates a movement, without any intention of completing it, merely in order to evoke the usual response from a companion. Such an uncompleted action is a gesture, and gestures in this sense may be seen in the play and in the business activities of many animals. If the movements preliminary to attack suffice to put an adversary to flight, the hostile action becomes reduced to a mere aggressive attitude. If the respondent animal anticipates correctly the agent need go no further. What makes possible the development of language from such beginnings is the multiplication of opportunities for their use and their more conscious use.

Turning now to the second of the two learning processes, we may say: An observed situation or event, in itself indifferent, is seen to be the signal for some further event or new situation that is interesting, and then comes to elicit behaviour which is adapted, in anticipation, to the situation expected. When men are working together at a common task, they have reason to take an interest in one another's actions, and they have to learn to anticipate them. To anticipate an event means to be able to recognize its antecedents. The various manipulations involved in hunting, fishing, preparing food, may be recognized at the first movement by anyone who is familiar with them. All mammals can anticipate, by observing one movement of another animal, what he is likely to do next. At certain hours of the day, when a walk or meal is in prospect, Sarah will take up her position in a corner from which she can observe me and watch my every movement with the closest attention. It can hardly be of much concern to her what clothes I wear, but when I issue from the lobby with a raincoat on, she immediately makes preparations for a walk. Thus when some action of mine (in itself indifferent to her) can be recognized as the prelude to something to which a reaction on her part is possible, she can assume some kind of preliminary stance, so that when the situation develops her reaction can be immediate. After lunch I have a nap, and about 3 p.m. Sarah, who can hardly be suspected of reading the clock, comes and puts both paws on my chest and breathes heavily in my face. If I tell her to lie down, she obeys for ten minutes and then repeats her gesture. This continues until I rise and prepare for our afternoon walk. The situation which prompts her action is me asleep in the armchair and the passage of some three quarters of an hour since the end of washing up the lunch things. This situation in itself can be of no interest to her except as a signal of what is to follow. She must have learned to recognize this premonitory situation and to adapt her behaviour in anticipation to the significant situation that is to follow. Communication in this case consists in her interpretation of my executive actions.

At the earliest stage the act of communication will differ little from the executive act from which it is derived. This most primitive type may be called *concrete* communication, and consists of actions deliberately used to convey to companions just what they might be expected to convey if used as executive acts. And since the meaning of any communicative act, at this stage, must depend on the exact circumstances in which it occurs and on the relations between agent and respondent, all communication must at first be improvised and closely related to the context. But gradually, we must suppose, actions which are intended and recognized as essentially communicative will be adapted in various ways for their special function, and we have to inquire how such adaptation could occur and what forms it assumed. The first step is towards the differentiation of specific signs, of actions which serve no executive purpose, but convey information or warning or command. Such signs, we saw, may arise from the simple abridgement of the executive act.

We shall see in the next chapter how this specialization may be supposed to have taken place. But there is one important condition which underlies the whole development and which must be briefly mentioned at this point. The activity of many men on the same task, performing the same actions, sharing the same experiences, must have encouraged each individual to compare his own body and actions with those of his companions. This comparison should not be taken for granted. Normally an animal behaves in the same way to like objects and differently to unlike ones, so that in dealing with other animals of one and the same species its behaviour will be uniform. In general this will be true also of its behaviour towards other members of its own species. On the basis of this common attitude to similar things we may say that the animal *recognizes* the resemblance. In this sense, however, it is certain that very few animals can recognize the resemblance between other members of their own species and themselves. An animal's relation to its own legs and tail is very different from its relation to the legs and tail even of its twin brother. And we could only infer such recognition from the fact that both evoked the same reactions. All conscious imitation implies some degree of identification of oneself with the other party (see below, Chapter 4). In this sense, however, it is doubtful to what extent even the higher apes can recognize the resemblance between other members of their own species and themselves. Even in man this power is not always well developed, and there must have been a time when it was hardly developed at all.

For want of a better expression I shall refer to this power which men acquire of comparing their own bodies with the bodies of their fellows as the *ego-alter association*. It will be discussed more fully later in connexion with the subject of imitation. Its relevance to concrete communication is fairly obvious, for every man in a social group must play the part of agent and respondent in turn, and the adoption of a common method by all will make for economy and clarity. Without a common method each man would use a different set of signs when acting as agent and have to understand all the different signs used by others. To give an analogy from modern conditions, since one may understand a foreign language and yet have difficulty in using it, a Frenchman and a German may converse together, each speaking his own language. So in the early stages of communication each man would develop his own mode of expressing himself and yet learn to understand the signs of all his companions. And in the absence of the ego-alter association it seems that this state of affairs would be almost inevitable, since all ground for recognizing a relation between the muscular action of making a sign and the visual experience of seeing one would be wanting. Of course, since the members of a community have similar resources and are in general subject to similar conditions, we might expect a general similarity in the signs used, but there is no reason why it should be close or extend to details. It is the ego-alter association which tends to produce a common system of communication among the members of a co-operating group. And we may say, perhaps, that the most important condition for progress towards a real language was that agent and respondent should be able to put themselves in the position one of the other, that the agent in devising methods of influencing the respondent should bethink him of the signs by which he, when acting as respondent, was or might be himself influenced; and that the respondent in trying to divine the meaning of the agent's signals should be able to refer to his own methods as agent in like circumstances.

As to how this wider conception of man, which resulted from the merging of the idea of self and the idea of objective man, was achieved, it may suffice for the present to say that co-operation on a large scale must continually provide examples of one and the same action seen under the two aspects, as performed by oneself and as performed by another, yet leading to the same objective consequences. And it seems obvious that any considerable ability to consider human actions under these two aspects can have been made possible only by social habits. But the ability was in turn, no doubt, one of the most important conditions for the further development of co-operation.

We cannot expect to find it easy to reconstruct this transitional stage in behaviour where the two independent phases of agent and respondent are merging into a reciprocal relation. The beginnings of such a situation can be discerned in the behaviour of chimpanzees. Rensch (p. 35) mentions experiments in which two chimpanzees learned to drag a food box (too heavy to be moved by a single animal) to the bars of their cage by pulling in co-operation on two ropes. When one animal pulled on one rope and failed to move the box, he indicated — by noises, gestures or pushing — that he wanted his cage mate to help by pulling on the other rope.

It has often been argued that men could never have felt the need for language before they possessed one, since they could not want something of which they could form no conception. It is true that the imagination can only extend and improve a little the realities already known and must progress by short experimental steps. But early man, struggling to improve his facility of communication, could go forward through stages of trial and error to construct a system which he had not, at the outset, foreseen, and which yet met his need so perfectly as to seem miraculous; for in retrospect we do not observe the multitude of steps and only see the transformation at the end. In the next chapter I shall try to trace some of the steps by which the invention of communicative signs was achieved.

CHAPTER 3

The Development of Signs

The principle which underlies the development of communication may be stated as follows: certain executive actions performed under social conditions are observed by those who perform them to produce secondary effects on other members of the community, and they are thereafter used deliberately for the sake of those effects. Among animals which live in society with man such communication develops to a limited extent. But before any kind of *system* could be formed from such actions, differentiation was necessary and communicative acts had to be specialized. We must now consider the conditions which led to such specialization.

Before any executive act can be exploited as a sign it must have a meaning which is understood by observers. The action must be familiar enough in its setting for its sequel and antecedents to be suggested. The word 'meaning' may seem a rather dangerous one to rely on in such a context, but every action may be said to have a 'meaning', in the same sense that this may be said of all the familiar phenomena of nature. The thundercloud means a coming storm, the drenched ground that there has been a downpour; the opening of the leafbuds that spring is at hand; the smoke clouds and crackle of burning wood that the forest is ablaze. And so, too, the groans, the cries and the laughter of men and women mean that they are in trouble, excited or glad. Every perceptible bodily movement means, for one who understands it, the purpose which it implies or the sequel which usually follows it. And the surviving traces of human activity, the marks of the axe, the embers of the fire, the footprints in the snow, mean the actions themselves, the actors, their purposes or their circumstances, in short everything that may be inferred from them.

These are the *natural* meanings of things, human or non-human. They are meanings, of course, only for those who can understand them, but they depend only on experience and not on any convention. But when a man acts for the purpose of conveying information, though he may perform the same actions, their meaning is not the same. The groan which is intended to convey some message or elicit some response is, to some extent at least, a simulated groan. It is not the spontaneous expression of feeling, and therefore the existence of that feeling is not to be inferred from it. The axe marks put on the tree for a sign must not be interpreted as if they resulted from an unsuccessful attempt to fell the tree. When the executive act becomes a sign its meaning undergoes a change. Yet the new meaning, the meaning of the sign, must always be derived from, and bear some intelligible relation to, the meaning of the act. But since the meaning of the act includes everything that may conceivably be inferred from it, the meaning of the sign must be much restricted if it is not to be ambiguous. Footprints mean that a man has passed. Their shape may reveal the direction he has taken, his speed, build, and even his identity. The extent of the meaning depends on the interest and the discernment of the observer. But when a footprint is deliberately made to convey a warning or an instruction, only some small part of all this can be intended. Thus, if a sign is to be effective its meaning must be restricted. And if we distinguish the *natural* meaning and the *sign* meaning of an action, we may say that while the sign meaning is primitively *derived* from the natural meaning it can *correspond* only to a part of it.

Every familiar action might thus be adapted for use as a sign, but there are certain other conditions required to make it suitable for specialization. To be effective as a mode of communication the action must be not only significant but readily perceived and easily performed. To be perceived it must be able to affect one of the respondent's senses. Taste and smell are excluded because they cannot be excited by any simple voluntary action. Touch involves contact and can serve only under very special circumstances. It has been made the basis of a form of communication by means of special devices, but the methods employed are secondary and based on oral language. We are thus left with hearing and vision. All natural forms of communication, therefore, depend on audible utterance or visible signs. Of the latter we must distinguish two kinds, those which are seen when they are performed, and those which are effective only through some durable trace which they leave behind.

These three types of sign, the audible, the visible and the durable, correspond approximately to speech, gesture and writing. But these, as we know them, are all highly conventional and of comparatively late origin. If we go back to the primitive stage of concrete communication we see that these three possibilities must have been represented by natural cries, pantomime and the normal physical effects of action. At a later stage we find evidence of imitation, and this will be considered in Chapter 4.

On the principle of the re-adaptation of responses it is easy to see how a natural cry or an emotional gesture could come to be exploited as a sign. The cry and the gesture are familiar to the respondent and may easily provoke him to some kind of response which the agent observes. But on the same principle it is not so easy to see how other sounds and other movements should ever come to be imitated. The agent may be said to imitate his own natural interjections when he employs them deliberately, and this kind of imitation involves merely repetition with a new purpose. But how can we suppose that a man should ever think of imitating the cry of an owl? What executive act can have given rise to such a sign?

Before coming to the discussion of the psychological basis of imitation it will be as well to review some of the forms which it takes in primitive methods of communication. We may take in turn the three modes already referred to—audible, visible, and durable. The first has come to be so much the most important that philosophers have often spoken as if oral language were the only real language; the whole problem of the origin of language has sometimes been treated as if it were the same as that of the origin of conventional speech, and this has led to some strange theories. In order to explain how we are able to express all our ideas by words, Herder maintained that all things have their natural sounds, and he seems to have supposed that the invention of language consisted merely in

the discovery of the natural sounds of all the objects and processes in the world. But any serious attempt to find characteristic noises for more than an almost negligible proportion of
the things in which man was naturally interested will show the
insufficience of such a theory. It is, of course, human beings
and other animals that lend themselves most readily to this
kind of representation, either on account of their voice or of
the noises produced by their various activities. But even here
the scope is very limited. It is true that some onomatopoeia
and sound-symbolism are to be found in most languages, but
the amount is relatively unimportant and, as we shall see later,
the phenomenon has a secondary origin. Thus, imitation can
provide but a small number of audible signs to add to those
which can have been directly adapted from pre-existing vocal
responses, and the oral languages which have been universal in
all historical times cannot owe their origin to the imitation of
natural sounds, whether human or otherwise.

We come to visible signs. We can here again draw the same
distinction between imitation of a man's own actions for the
purpose of communication and imitation of the actions of
other men, of animals and other objects. In both categories
the possibilities are far greater than in the case of sounds. A
man's voice accounts for only a fraction of his behaviour. Of
all the things which he may do and which may have an interest
for his fellows, the vast majority are visible and recognizable
when seen, and only an almost negligible minority are audible
or, if audible, recognizable from the sound. Hence it was
inevitable that at first efforts at communication should appeal
primarily to the eye. Conventional forms of language can,
of course, appeal to any of the senses, but conventional forms
of language can only have arisen on the basis of a natural
language, and we have to explain this before we can hope to
understand that.

The language of movement is sometimes referred to as the
gesture-language. But the gesture-language which is practised
by the deaf and dumb, and by the North American Indians
and others, is in many respects highly conventional. The primitive language of movement must have consisted at first of all
kinds of representative actions, not only those very restricted
facial and digital movements commonly associated with the

word 'gesture'. Pantomime would be a more suggestive term. But let us consider some of the forms which it takes. We have seen that although the sign meaning of an action is more restricted than its natural meaning, yet any portion of the latter may furnish the sign meaning. In the gesture-languages actually in use we find that actions are used continually to indicate not only the actions themselves, but also their aim, their method or their result. Most actions involve some part of the material environment, and often they cannot be imitated without reference to a material object, person or substance, which is affected by the action. And the action, as sign, may be used to suggest any of these associated objects or effects. Thus the action of drinking may signify the desire to drink, an invitation to drink, a drinking vessel, or simply water. The action of digging may signify the action itself, the spade, the hole, or any other of the possible aspects or purposes of the operation. This variety of possible interpretations, provided the difficulty of ambiguity can be overcome, makes one sign serve for a number of ideas.

Now just as it is possible by performing an action to suggest an object, so by calling attention to an object one may sometimes suggest an action. If the object is present it may be indicated by touching, pointing, handling. In the presence of a shared situation communication about the details of that situation will often depend on such reference to accessible objects. Sometimes object and action may be combined; but if the object is not available or the action is not easy, one part of the complex will do duty for the other. A picture, if it is available, is often the most adequate representation that can be given of a material object; and pictures of a kind can be quickly made in the sand or on any soft surface. Models may be even better, but are generally harder to make. The idea of a tool may be suggested by an appropriate movement with the hands. But this may be made clearer if, in the absence of the real tool, some object that resembles it is held in the hands. The substitute may be improved to increase the likeness and then we have a form of imitation. Actions of animals may be imitated, either with the whole body or by movements of the arms or fingers. Such imitative actions may be made more realistic with the aid of various properties, furnishings or dress. Here again there may be an attempt to imitate not only the action but the appearance of the animal. And, of course, where animals are concerned, the imitative actions can be reinforced by imitative noises.

The use of objects, whether natural or imitated, for communication brings us to the third class of signs, those that are durable. They are usually employed in addressing not a present but a future respondent. In conversing with a companion it is as easy to use one's foot or one's finger as one's footprint or fingermark. For the *result* of an action is effective as a sign only where the connexion between action and result is familiar, and where this is so nothing will be conveyed to a present audience by display of the result, which is not equally clearly conveyed by the action. But as a means of communication to persons not present (i.e. of sending messages) such durable marks or concrete objects are the only signs available.

Any action which leaves a recognizable trace may be used for this type of communication. The simplest case, perhaps, in which we can recognize the re-adaptation of an executive act is the device of blazing a trail. Most animals that move on the ground leave some kind of trail, and this is made use of either by their enemies or by their own kind. Man also leaves involuntary tracks, but he, observing their effect on the behaviour of his companions, takes measures to make them more lasting and conspicuous. Comparing such experiences with those in which he is himself the tracker, he enlarges his idea of the significance of such traces, whether of animals or men. Such durable signs made upon the ground or on the more permanent environmental features, are found to serve not only as a signal to others but as a future guide to him who makes them. These, it may be noted, are the chief uses of writing: to convey information to others not present, and to record information for one's own future use.

The first stage in the development of language was *concrete communication* (cf. above, p. 16), when there are no specialized signs, but the normal actions of men engaged on co-operative tasks are modified somewhat with the secondary purpose of influencing the behaviour of companions and facilitating co-operation. In the second stage signs have become specialized, and there is a clear distinction between an executive act and a communicative act, so that the one is not easily mistaken for the other. At this stage signs are still of all kinds—facial expressions, vocal sounds, actions or objects, or any combination of these. This may be refered to as *primitive sign communication*. These two stages are not, of course, represented in any known community today, or recorded in historical times, and are therefore theoretical. The third stage is one of gradual differentiation of methods. The gesture-languages are developed as essentially manual and facial languages, their dependence on real objects disappearing through the fixing of conventions. Full-scale dramatic representations are replaced by brief conventionalized movements. The picture-language is developed for distant communication and comes to depend entirely on the two-dimensional representation of objects, conventionally simplified, and assisted by purely conventional symbols.

The history of the development of language may be said to be concerned with this gradual process of conventionalization. But conventional signs imply natural ones, and they can be developed only from or with the aid of the latter. Intermediate between the primitive sign communication, in which self-explanatory pantomime was an almost essential ingredient, and purely conventional language came imitative signs, on which basis a great extension in the scope of communication occurred. But this use of imitative signs should not be taken for granted, and we have to explain how it could arise.

Vocal language depends on the introduction of conventions and taxes the memory more than other modes of communication because in a language of sounds it is difficult to retain any palpable associative link between sign and meaning, such as is usually possible both in picture-writing and in gesture-language. The idea that conventional sound languages are ultimately to be derived from communication by means of self-explanatory gestures is today widely regarded as discredited.[1] Jespersen, who devotes a chapter to the origin of language, does not even mention the possibility that gesture may

---

1.   Hewes, however, impressed by the results achieved by the Gardners and others in teaching conventional gestures to chimpanzees, is a notable exception (Eds.).

have had something to do with it. One reason for this is that those earlier writers (e.g. Tylor and Wundt) who took most seriously the theory that spoken language was preceded by gesture-language, formed their notion of the latter from a study of the languages of the deaf and dumb, and similar conventional systems. But the primitive sign communication must have been very different. At this stage men knew how to distinguish a sign from an executive act, and they had learnt to employ all kinds of methods to express their desires and convey information, but they had not reduced any one method to a conventional system. We may to some extent determine *a priori* the methods which would be at their disposal, but we have no direct means of finding out which of these methods were in fact made use of. There is however an indirect means, which I attempted to employ in a series of experiments which will be described in a later chapter. Children, brought up in the usual way, having no knowledge of any conventional gesture-language and no notions at all about the theory of communication, may be reduced artificially to the condition of dependence on signs instead of language. My aim was to prevent as far as possible the use of all conventional signs and see how children, under such a restriction, would set about conveying ideas to one another. The result was, as might be expected, something very different from the conventional language of the deaf and dumb.

An exception to the usual neglect of gesture as an important factor in the origin of human speech is Paget's book of 1930. I shall show below that the hypothesis he offers in order to fill the gap between self-explanatory gesture and conventional sound is implausible, and has therefore further discredited the idea that the latter can be derived from the former. My own proposal for bridging this crucial gap is that the impulse to the development of oral language may well have been given by the increased conventionalization gradually introduced into other forms of communication. I shall discuss the subject in detail in a later chapter, but a brief summary is appropriate at this point. If communication originated with the development of a self-explanatory gesture-language; if in time many signs became reduced until they were no longer self-explanatory, and could not be understood by outsiders, then — sooner or later —

someone would realize that, since purely arbitrary (i.e. not in any way self-explanatory) signs could serve perfectly well for communication between members of the same group, arbitrary sounds were as good as any other arbitrary signs, and had many advantages of their own. In the second place, proper names are apt to be too numerous for gestural methods. It is hardly possible that names could be given to every member of a large community which should carry any suggestiveness to aid the memory. Dogs in general may be known as bow-wows, but on a similar principle it would be impossible to find different names for very many individuals, whether the name is a sound or any other kind of sign. Hence conventional signs for individuals became inevitable, and since they must be conventional, sound would have no disadvantage as compared with gesture.

Before going on to deal in greater detail with the gesture-language and the picture-language, I shall try to explain certain general principles which will have frequent application in what follows, namely imitation, conventionalization and symbolism.

CHAPTER 4

Imitation

The principle of imitation is often appealed to in explanation both of animal behaviour and of human cultural development. But as an explanatory principle it remains unsatisfactory as long as it is itself not clearly understood. Psychologists have sometimes spoken of an imitative instinct. William James includes it in his long list of instincts. But although in many animals there may be instinctive responses which are imitative in character, they are specific. The sheep may jump or the dog bark when it sees or hears its neighbour do so, but it does not copy every action performed by another member of its species. In the case of man, the arch-imitator, it is open to doubt whether instinctive imitation occurs, at any rate after infancy; and in what follows I hope to show that even if it did, it would not be of the least help in explaining the origins of human communication.

In the first place, we must draw a clear distinction between imitation of an *action* and of an *effect*. Both types may be illustrated in the instinctive behaviour of birds. In some species it appears that the chicks do not begin to peck for grain until they have observed the pecking procedure of the older birds. Here, the chick is imitating the *action* of its elder. On the other hand, the parrot, when it imitates the human voice, is imitating the effect. The difference between the two situations is clear. The chick sees the older bird, and follows its example, but is in no position to observe itself and compare its own action with that of its parent. The parrot cannot observe the movements of the human vocal apparatus; it reproduces the human sounds with a very different apparatus of its own. But it is in a position to compare the imitated sound with the original one, and no doubt is able to improve its performance after repetition. In general terms, when an animal repeats the actions of another animal with its own body there is no possibility of any direct comparison between the model and the copy except by a neutral observer. But where the action copied produces some audible or visible effect distinct from the movement itself, then this effect may be accessible to the senses of both animals on equal terms, and each animal is able to compare the effect of his own action with that of the other animal's action. Where this effect is a sound, it is only requisite that the animal should have a hearing apparatus.

In his discussion of imitation in apes, Köhler stresses the importance of *understanding* what one is imitating. Apes can imitate one another in actions which are part of their common repertoire, but they cannot imitate an action which is new to them. Köhler says that if an ape is faced with a problem which it cannot solve by its own resources it will very seldom benefit from seeing it solved by another, and can do so 'only when the situation and its solution lie roughly within the limits drawn for the spontaneous solution also' (p. 160).[1] Clearly, the behaviour which Köhler is discussing is of a very different kind from that of either the pecking chicks or the talking parrot. There is here no question of instinctive mimicry. The animal is motivated by a quest for food, and its movements are designed to reproduce not the movements of its teacher, but their results. It is imitation of this kind, regarded by Köhler as a rarity in animals, which is such a conspicuous talent in man; an imitation made possible by an understanding of the situation, and motivated by a desire for a particular result.

In many cases, the result is achieved only after careful observation of another man's action. But we may also imitate the result of an action without observing the action, either because we know from experience how it is done, or because we set about experimenting in order to find out. If we do not know and cannot find out we must watch the process and endeavour to repeat it. But this is only possible in certain conditions, as is easily illustrated. A man, liking a tune he hears played on the

---

1. More recent work has, on the whole, endorsed Köhler's scepticism. Spence, for instance, is very critical (p. 821) of the view that animals are capable of conscious imitation (Eds.).

piano, tries to play it himself. If he is able to do so he is certainly not imitating the movements of the original pianist, but reproducing the effect by means already at his command. In the same way we see students in our art galleries copying the works of the masters. They do not try to imitate the actual movements of the original artist.

In these cases it is not the movements that are copied, but the actions as understood. If one boy kicks a football, another boy can imitate his performance because he has it already in his repertoire. If one man pronounces an intelligible sentence in English, an Englishman will be able to imitate him, or rather to repeat the sentence. The words of our own language are known to us under many aspects, more particularly as audible impressions when pronounced by another and as muscular sensations when pronounced by ourselves. These two aspects are linked by experience and constant use, as any two aspects of a familiar object are linked. We can, therefore, pronounce a word at will and on hearing a word we can if we wish repeat it. In many imitative actions, then, the response is indirect. It is the meaning of the action that is understood and it is this meaning that is then freshly expressed. If the two parties have learned to express their ideas in the same way the result will seem like imitation. But there is no direct imitation of movement; there is first a recognition of what the movement as a whole signifies — e.g. kicking a ball or blowing one's nose — and then an independent action to express it. Actions without apparent meaning, however, can be copied only by an attempt to reproduce the precise sequence of muscular movements.

It is evident that the imitation of an action involves the *ego-alter* association (cf. p. 17 above); for if a man can make his body perform in detail the movements which he sees performed by another body without having preconceived ideas of the movements in question, then he must be able to translate or transform the visual impressions which he receives of those movements into the corresponding muscular reactions. And this means either that there exists in the brain a transforming system which automatically connects the visual image of the action, as seen, with the effector complex which issues in the action itself; or that the required association must be established little by little, first for one movement and then for another, so that the possibility of imitation is always limited to particular learned actions. The number of these may be very large, but all must be acquired specially. The former alternative seems inconceivable. If we ask how some particular movement — e.g. the action of kneeling on one knee — appears to an observer who has, to start with, no idea of it; and if we consider only the sequence of visual images which he receives, as in a series of frames in a cine-film: then it is obvious that this series will be quite different according to his position in relation to the kneeler. If, therefore, the sight of the action is to provoke automatically the action itself, then the association which procures this result would have to lie between *every possible aspect* of the visible movement and the muscular response. Otherwise there must be some particular aspect which alone elicits the imitative reaction, and in other cases there can be no response.

It is surely evident that the imitation of such an action depends on the existence of an idea in the mind representing this movement both as seen and as performed, and only gradually constructed in the course of a man's bodily education. His own movement he knows principally through the mediation of his muscular sense, but he can associate with this whatever he can see of his own body during the movement, and in the case of movements in which different limbs come in contact with one another, the sensations of touch and pressure. This complex of sensations has no resemblance at all to the complex which represents the same movement as seen in another, and the latter, which is mainly visual, differs very considerably according to the relative positions of actor and observer. Hence, if a man is to have a fairly adequate idea of such a movement, he must link together in his mind all these various impressions in a single comprehensive idea, and this idea will, of course, be linked with all kinds of situations and reactions. The action may occur in response to the visual aspect of the action itself and in that case we have imitation. But such an imitative response does not occur automatically or spontaneously but only in intelligent relation to a wider situation. We try to imitate an instructor because we wish to do what he can do; we imitate the actions of a man because we see that they lead him into a situation which we too should like to occupy. We may not fully realize our motives, and they may even be suppressed, but imitation does not occur without a motive.

Even if we were to assume the existence in man of a natural tendency or impulse to respond imitatively to the movements or actions of other men, we should not be much nearer to understanding the role of imitation in language. If a man imitates the sound of water or the cry of an animal in order to suggest these things to his companion, this is a rational act which has nothing to do with any impulsive response to a like stimulus. If we suppose that the sound of water gives rise to an impulse to hiss or bubble, we still cannot explain how hissing and bubbling came to be deliberately employed, in the absence of water, to suggest the idea of water. If the sight of an animal naturally excites a man to imitate its form by drawing on a rock, this alone will not explain the use of drawings to suggest the animal when it is not present. But whereas the imitative instinct, so often invoked in this connexion, cannot be taken for granted, we can at least be certain that there is in humans—as to a lesser extent in other animals—a remarkable imitative *ability;* the instinct, if it exists, can do little more than make its possessor aware of his own talents.

In order to understand how this particular talent came to be used for the purpose of communication, we must return to the fundamental principle of the re-adaptation of reactions. How did conscious imitative reactions arise, and how could they produce effects which might lead to their re-adaptation for the purpose of communication? We shall start with the imitation of human actions. If A were to observe in B any tendency to repeat A's movements, and if on any occasion he should wish B to act in a certain way, then A might himself deliberately set the example in order to elicit the desired behaviour. But we have first to discover under what circumstances B would show such an imitative tendency. In such a case the agent is not employing imitation himself but exploiting the observed imitative behaviour of the respondent. The principle employed (setting an example) assumes in the respondent a tendency to follow the example set. Now the example of some individuals is eagerly followed, but most people have very little power of exciting imitators. The method is really effective only when the respondent recognizes the process and believes that he can gain some advantage from copying. And here we come again to the importance of co-operation. When agent and respondent are working in harmony the situation is favourable for communication by any means. If B is puzzled to know how to deal with a particular situation and if he is aware that A can show him, then the problem for A is comparatively simple. But the whole problem of communication has already been potentially solved when such a situation can easily arise. If A and B are both working for the same result and if A understands how they may achieve it, then if B is able to look to A for guidance and A is willing to provide this, it is obviously only a question of experiment to discover a means of communication. Imitative methods may then be supposed to develop in response to the recognized need. But the most important imitative methods do not arise out of the imitative action of the respondent. How does the agent himself come to make use of imitative methods, gestures, drawings or sounds employed to suggest some object or action other than that required of the respondent?

We may, perhaps, be able to trace a natural transition from the one to the other. Starting from the form of communication which consists in inducing the respondent to perform some action by demonstrating it to him, and which we may call *imperative* communication because it is designed to evoke a specific response rather than to convey information, then we have to show how this might gradually develop into *indicative* communication, where the aim of the agent is merely to make the respondent aware of certain facts. In the latter case the agent may use imitative methods to suggest ideas; he may suggest an animal by means of a drawing or by mimicking its cry.

Before trying to trace the connexion between the two types, I must introduce one other preliminary. Communication may be roughly divided into two categories: *colloquial and forensic*. The former occurs between persons who are face to face and in the presence of a common situation. Such communication may be experimental, since the agent can judge the success of his efforts from the demeanour of the respondent. When one sign is not understood another can be tried, and where a single sign does not suffice a sequence may serve. The nature of the signs used may be adapted to the immediate situation, and mutual understanding between parties greatly facilitates the process. Forensic communication, on the other hand, is employed where these advantages are lacking. Messages are usually couched in forensic language, for they must be so framed as to eliminate ambiguities and anticipate questions. The same is true of any public statement to a large audience, where no interchange is possible between the speaker and the individual listeners. A private letter to an individual must usually be more explicit than an oral communication, but this depends more on the community of ideas between the participants than on the geographical distance between them.

The difference between colloquial and forensic forms of language is related to that between imperative and indicative communication. In the beginning communication must be predominantly imperative; the agent wants something of the respondent and employs his signs to induce the desired action. Much can be accomplished of this kind with limited resources and with the aid of natural signs. In the presence of a shared situation agent and respondent have common interests and purposes, which make the aims of each the concern of the other. But when information has to be imparted which is only remotely connected with the actual situation, *representative* signs are needed, signs which have a constant meaning as far as possible independent of present circumstances. In colloquial language this constancy of meaning is less important than in forensic language, and in concrete communication (as defined in a previous chapter) it is unnecessary, for each sign gets its meaning from the environmental context apart from which it would have none.

How then did representative signs arise, how did descriptive or indicative communication develop out of imperative? At first sight there seems to be a gulf between the two. Animals, as we know, learn to respond appropriately to all kinds of complex situations, and there is no reason why they should not learn to respond to signs, sounds and gestures made by other animals. On the other hand animals learn to deal appropriately with their environment, to make use of objects and apply them to their own purposes, and there is no reason why they should not learn to make use of the reactions of other animals where these may be of use to them. Now imperative communication involves no more than this, the ability on the one hand to respond to a sign and on the other to make the sign for the sake of eliciting that response. But indicative communication does not necessarily involve any action at all on the part of the respondent, and therefore it does not seem explicable in the same way.

The rudiments of indicative communication can, however, be seen in the relation between man and dog. Sarah is quite capable of understanding the meaning of many of my actions which are not intended as communications at all. When I put my shoes on she knows that I am going out. When I turn off my electric radiator at a quarter to one Dinah knows that I am going down to get their dinner. What they actually do in such a case will depend on circumstances, though the uniformity of circumstances usually leads to much the same reactions. If Dinah believes there is a cat in the garden she is filled with indignation and conceives it to be her duty to go and drive it out. And it is only necessary to mention the hated word to her with a certain emphasis in order to call forth the usual reaction. This could be regarded as a response to a signal, but it is probable that the word gives rise in her mind to an idea and that it is this idea which evokes the reaction, for she acts in the same way on any kind of evidence of an intruding cat. After a meal Dinah and Sarah come and sit one on either side of me to receive a certain traditional ration of biscuits. They patiently receive what I have to give them and do not think of going away until I tell them that there is no more. But as soon as I say this they get up and go away. Here again it might seem that this is merely a reaction to a signal. But the reaction is not constant so far as its positive content is concerned. Dinah will sometimes just lie down. Sarah may go to her favourite corner or prowl around or challenge Dinah to a game. All that is clear is that she expects no more biscuits. My words are not even necessary, for it is enough for me to fold up my serviette and put it in its ring, or even to put the lid on the biscuit barrel. From any of these actions they judge that the session is concluded and that they may as well go about their other business. It may therefore be said that my words or gestures

are not imperative in effect but indicative. They do not command any particular action, they merely give information on
which the respondents may act according to their judgment.
When we are out walking in the wood and come to a forked
path, Sarah, who is always far ahead, stops and watches my
movements to see whether they incline to the right or left. As
soon as she judges from my movements which path I am going
to take, she turns and scampers on. I do not have to give any
signal. But if I did it would certainly not act as a compelling
stimulus, since she knows very well that she is free to run where
she will, and she has never learnt to be directed in her movements like a sheep-dog. If my movements cause her to take one
path rather than the other it is merely because they inform her
of my intentions, and because although she does not mind
which path we take she prefers that we should go together.

Here then we have indicative communication, but the
information conveyed concerns actions and situations closely
related to actions. How can we explain the transition to the use
of representative signs, imitative or symbolical signs which
somehow awaken in the mind of the respondent the idea of
certain objects or conditions which are not only not present,
but towards which no immediate reaction from him is required? The answer will be given in greater detail in later
chapters, but it may be briefly indicated here. A gesture, a
movement of the body, naturally suggests to the observer the
action it resembles and the observer, if he has any interest in
the matter, responds appropriately according to the way in
which he interprets it. But many actions cannot be performed
except in relation to other objects, tools, materials. The action
of sawing performed in vacuo, so to speak, would be
ambiguous or even quite unintelligible. But if it is performed
with any kind of object in the hand on some other fixed piece
of material the meaning is at once clear. Thus gestures are
supplemented by dummies and substitutes. And the latter may
easily become the signs for the objects they represent. All that
is then required is an improvement in the representation. Such
dummies need not be exact copies of the things they represent,
since they are explained by the action which accompanies
them. But if they are to be used *instead* of such action they
must either suggest their meaning by their likeness or they

must have acquired a meaning by convention. Communication by means of dummies is obviously impracticable and such methods can only have supplemented more rapid forms. One cannot carry about a sack of conversational materials like the professors of Laputa. But for a number of things the hands may be used as a model and we find this method freely adopted by the deaf and dumb. Even more important for some forms of communication is the substitution of two-dimensional drawings for models. How far such methods can have been effective and what their limitations are, we shall see later. Neither drawings nor models nor any other concrete representations of objects could provide a comprehensive means for colloquial communication; but they could be employed in special circumstances where other methods failed, and we find them in fact both in the gesture-language of the deaf and dumb and in picture-writing.

CHAPTER 5

Convention and Symbolism

When it is said that a sign is conventional, the meaning may be that it is standardized, streamlined, stylized or arbitrary. *Standardization* means the replacement of a number of variant forms by one agreed form, which need not be better, clearer or more concise than any other of those previously used, but which is chosen for the sake of the advantages offered by uniformity. *Streamlining* means that a form is reduced and simplified so that it is easier to make. Such streamlining may be made by many individuals independently and lead to divergence in usage, but it may also be standardized. *Stylization* may involve some elaboration as well as simplification. An *arbitrary* sign is usually contrasted with one that is self-explanatory. Streamlined and stylized signs tend to become arbitrary, though they are not always so.

Standardization has two purposes or advantages. First, the individual writer or speaker is freed from the hesitation and mental exertion required by any choice. Speed and accuracy in writing or speaking, as in any other operation, can be attained only if the movements practised are uniform, and if random ones are eliminated. If there are half a dozen different ways of forming a letter, there will be a tendency to pause and consider every time it has to be written, and the practice gained will be six times less. Second, standardization aids mutual understanding. If different writers or speakers use a different vocabulary or different characters, although each may keep strictly to one for his own use, he must still be able to understand them all. In a particular society there are of course very often smaller groups within which special signs are used not intelligible outside the group. But in any community whose members are in constant intercommunication signs will

tend to become standardized. There are certain counter-
vailing psychological factors which make for individual idio-
syncrasies, but a limit is set by the need for mutual compre-
hension.

Streamlining serves the purposes of speed and facility. A
sign when first employed may be more elaborate than necessary and experience may show that it may be simplified without
disadvantage. The mere fact that it has come into general
use allows a reduction to be made without loss of understanding. The abridged sign would perhaps convey nothing at all
if used for the first time, but a gradual reduction which
proceeds as the sign grows more familiar is generally possible.
Such reduction may finally result in a sign which is quite
arbitrary in form. The most familiar and striking example of
such streamlining is to be seen in the development of Egyptian
writing, of which something will be said later. But streamlining occurs at all stages and does not necessarily result in
completely arbitrary symbols. Here again a limit is set by the
need for mutual understanding. However useful it is to write
and speak easily and quickly, it is still desirable to be understood. Where a secret language is required, other methods
than streamlining are available to disguise the symbols or
conceal their meaning.

Stylizing means any kind of elaboration of signs for any
purpose other than facilitating use and increasing intelligibility. But perhaps we may include under the same heading
some of the methods adopted to counteract the effects of over-
simplification. The latter tends to bring about the assimilation of distinct signs. If this causes misunderstanding new
methods must be employed to discriminate, and as a result
the signs are elaborated in some way. In oral language this is
known to philologists as dissimilation. Another motive which
leads to stylizing is the artistic pleasure of the user of signs.
Whatever activity requires skill for its performance becomes
pleasurable to the skilful performer, and in this way many
kinds of craft develop into art. Religious motives may produce
a similar result. The sacred character of the material to be
spoken or written seems to demand a specially dignified
manner.

Finally we distinguish arbitrary signs (those which owe their meaning only to convention) from natural ones, which are self-explanatory. In order to explain the origin and development of language the two chief questions we have to answer are, what natural signs formed the starting point, and how these came to be replaced by arbitrary signs.

Like convention and imitation, symbolism is so familiar that we are apt to take it for granted and assume the use of a sign has been explained when its symbolical character has been shown. It is however always advisable to inquire carefully into what seem obvious forms of behaviour, especially when much explanatory theorizing is founded on them.

Wundt distinguishes between representative and symbolic gestures. An action or an object may be directly represented by an imitation of the action or a copy of the object, as when in Egyption hieroglyphics the *ibis* is represented by a picture of the bird. But the picture of an ibis bending forward in the act of seizing some interesting morsel, represents not the bird but the act of *finding* something, and is therefore a symbolic sign. If a particular action is naturally associated with a particular object, as drinking with water, or cutting with a knife, then either may be used as a symbolic gesture to suggest the other. A clenched fist may be used as the sign for 'hand', and it is in that case a direct representation; or it may be used as a symbol for aggression or challenge. The need for a symbolic sign is obvious where a quality has to be expressed, for one cannot convey the idea of *green* or *sweet* or *heavy* without some reference to an object possessing the quality, even though one's purpose does not concern that object.

It is easy to see how this kind of indirect representation arises. Actions and objects are apt to be closely associated, the one inevitably suggesting the other. Chopping suggests an axe, eating suggests food, drawing a bow suggests the arrow. The gesture can indeed convey no meaning unless the imagination of the respondent can supply the implied object, and conversely the concrete representation of such tools or weapons means nothing to one who cannot imagine them in use.

The *natural* meaning, as we have seen, of any action is *all* that it may imply for an observer, and its *sign* meaning may be any of these possible implications. The same action may thus express many things according to circumstances, and it is not always possible to say what it represents most directly. It appears therefore that from the first, symbolic representation is inevitable. We have become used to analysing our ideas into units according to the words we have. But an idea is not a natural aggregate of simple components, out of which its representation can be compiled. It can in any case only be suggested more or less plausibly. The gesture or picture employed can at best represent it only partially, though, if successful, it may evoke in the mind of the respondent a perfectly adequate idea. By whatever criterion we decide what is *directly represented*, more than this must almost always be *conveyed*. And to this extent every sign is symbolic, so that some degree of symbolization is involved in all communication.

To begin with, of course, such symbolism is not deliberate, it is merely the result of the inevitable ambiguity of all signs. Men did not first conceive the notion of using symbols and then exercise their ingenuity in devising effective ones. They were compelled by lack of conventions and the need for improvisation to approximate to their meaning by whatever actions suggested themselves; they observed the effect of their efforts and learnt by experience. Thus the behaviour of the agent was characterized by trial and error, and the habits which became established were determined by the reactions of the respondent.

We may attempt to classify the relations commonly existing between what is actually represented and what is suggested, but of course where convention is involved there need no longer be any definable relation at all. Such classification can hardly be said to have much scientific significance, and one could no doubt extend the number of categories indefinitely. But the following list will serve to call attention to the analogy between methods used in the gesture-language of the deaf and dumb (from which the examples are taken) and the common metaphors of oral language.

The part for the whole. Closed hand on breast to denote 'woman'. Representation of antlers with the hands to denote 'stag'.

Cause for effect. Touching the ear or tongue to denote

'to hear' or 'to taste'.

Effect for cause. Putting the hands to the lower ribs and showing how the heart flutters and seems to rise to the throat to denote 'fear'.

Object for action. Touching the ear or tongue, as above.

Action for product. Grinding fists together to denote 'corn'.

Manipulation for object. Action of spreading or sprinkling to denote 'butter' or 'salt'.

Object for quality. Lips to denote 'red', and pointing to or making the sign for grass to denote 'green'.

One object to denote another similar object. Cupping the hands to denote 'bowl' or 'drinking vessel'.

The same type of symbolism can be illustrated by examples in every kind of communication. But it is plain that each particular form — gesture, picture or sound — is better adapted for the representation of one kind of thing. Objects are more easily represented by pictures, actions and movements by gestures.

As soon as any sign has acquired a conventional meaning it may be used to denote all kinds of other related ideas. The representation may thus become more and more indirect. The transfer of meaning may continue indefinitely, provided only one step is taken at a time. If the first experimental use of a symbol succeeds it may be adopted as a conventional sign. Thenceforward it has the status of a direct representation and may be used symbolically for something else. Grammarians sometimes distinguish between live and dead metaphor. The former is experimental, an improvisation intended to convey something that cannot be conveyed directly. If it is successful in suggesting the new meaning it is repeated and gradually assumes that new meaning instead of its old one. It is then a dead metaphor, so long as anybody can still remember its former meaning, and when this is forgotten it is no longer a metaphor.

Even where purely conventional signs are used, as in oral language, the meaning is never so precise that it does not suggest somewhat different ideas to different hearers. When one man adopts for his own purpose a sign which he has first seen used by somebody else, he will employ it in the sense in which he understood it, and often this is not the sense in which it was used. This uncertainty of meaning must attach to nearly all signs except where the meaning is of a particularly simple nature. Ambiguity can only be avoided by multiplication. A number of alternative signs may be given for one and the same idea so that unwanted associations are eliminated. Or a group of different signs may be combined to convey a complex idea, and the respondent's knowledge enables him to see the meaning of each sign through the suggestiveness of the others. The word 'full' has many meanings but the addition of one more word will often determine the sense in which it is used, as a 'full moon', 'a full jug', 'a full heart', or 'a full skirt'. And so it is with every other kind of ambiguous sign when it is used in an intelligible context.

When the art of communication becomes more conscious, symbolic signs are deliberately adopted and their use may even become methodical. But the use of symbols does not always make for clearness or precision. On the contrary it may be merely a lax way of expressing one's ideas, or even a way of hiding one's lack of them. Sign-making, whether in the form of pantomime or painting or speaking, may serve chiefly for expressing emotion and not for the conveyance of any definite ideas. The signs are then determined only by their association with the emotion and by their mutual affinities. Such utterances may superficially simulate the forms of communication, but can be generally identified by their want of coherence. Where purely conventional signs are used this identification may be more difficult, and in the case of speech there is a broad region between intelligible discourse and emotional efflux where the two are mingled in uncertain proportions, and it is often hard for the listener to know whether a given sequence of words represents a valid idea or not. There are several possibilities. The agent may have valid ideas to convey but choose his signs so badly that they are misunderstood. Or the respondent may be ignorant of the signs used and so cannot interpret them. Or again, the agent's ideas may be clear and his signs appropriate, but the respondent may lack the mental capacity to reconstruct those ideas in his own mind. Finally, the agent may be trying to convey a mere muddle of incoherent thoughts and the more successful he is the more perplexed the respondent is likely to be.

It is important not to confuse *isolated* symbols or signs

(such as words) which are arbitrarily linked to certain things or ideas, with *systems* of symbols, where there is a correspondence between the whole system of relations connecting the symbols and the whole system of relations connecting the thing symbolized. 'Belle Vue' may be the name of only one house in the street and may therefore be taken as an unambiguous symbol for that house. And every house may have a name that symbolizes it in the same sense. But knowledge of these names will not tell us anything about the relative positions of the houses. On the other hand the numbers, since they are assigned according to an easily understood system, inform us directly concerning the positions of the houses. Thus the numbers form a system which is more than a mere collection of disconnected symbols. Experiments can be performed on such systems, the results of which are valid for the systems symbolized. With a map and a timetable we can make experimental voyages and draw conclusions about time, expense, fatigue and other matters which the real voyages are likely to involve. A system of co-ordinates is a more refined system of symbols than a set of numbers. From the arithmetical relations between two sets of co-ordinates we can infer the geometrical relations between two points. Mathematics is the most elaborate and efficient of all symbolic systems, whereas language, if it can be reckoned a system at all, is surely the most inadequate. Failure to appreciate this has led many writers into error both about language and about mathematics.

Every system of symbols must be related to a system which it symbolizes. The symbolic system consists in signs or tokens, with certain rules for their manipulation. Every sign or group of signs, and every specific operation provided in the system, must correspond in a definite way with some part of the system symbolized. Furthermore, the symbolic system must not be perfectly arbitrary, but such that, given any set of rules, no matter how chosen, definite consequences are deducible from them. And no such deduction is possible unless the symbols, by their own character and constitution, restrict and prescribe in some manner their feasible arrangements. A real set of symbols owes its value to the fact that it is subject, like the system of phenomena which it symbolizes, to the determinations of natural law. It is flexible, but only within limits, like a box of bricks or meccano set. The number of structures that can be made with a box of bricks may be large and their forms varied, but they are all deducible from the number and shape of the bricks given. And this is because the physical properties of the bricks — their mass, shape and persistent identity — are fixed. The value of a system of symbols is that the natural changes to which it is subject correspond to the natural changes in some other set of things which is less easily manipulated or explored. Plans, drawings and blueprints are symbolic representations of material structures. If they are useful, it is because one may confidently infer from correlations in the plan to correlations in the structure. From drawings we can only make inferences as to spatial disposition, not as to equilibria or strength of materials. Three-dimensional models of appropriate materials may permit inferences of other kinds. Mathematical symbols seem more remote from the things symbolized than models and drawings, but they are subject to the same conditions. They can be utilized only when a correspondence has been established between the possible manipulations of the symbols and dispositions of the things symbolized.

The word 'symbol' is now often used with a very wide meaning. Words, for example, are said to be the symbols of the ideas they stand for. But it will be obvious that in the sense in which I have used the word in the present chapter every conventional sign is not a symbol. In my usage the symbol is an indirect representation, one which acquires its representative virtue indirectly through its association with another sign. The sign 5 is not in this sense a symbol of the number, but a *hand* could be. Yet it will have become obvious that there can be no clear dividing line between one kind of representation and another, and it is this fact, no doubt, which has led to the use of the word 'symbol' as a synonym of the word 'sign'. The symbolism of which we have spoken hitherto is entirely unsystematic. All languages make use of symbols in the narrower sense, and, in the wider sense, consist entirely of symbols. But no language is a *system* of symbols like algebra, and one of the misconceptions which have arisen from the loose application of the word is the notion that language is, or can be made to be, a kind of universal mathematics. But to that extraordinary fallacy I shall return in a later chapter.

CHAPTER 6

Gesture-language

In order to find out how children, normally depending on speech, would improvise methods of expression if deprived temporarily of the conventional medium, I made a series of experiments on boys of various ages between 11 and 16. They were arranged in groups of two or three members. For each experiment one member of a group acted as agent and the remaining members as respondents. Only one group was present during an experiment. The procedure was as follows. The boy acting as agent received a slip of paper with a word written on it and was told to convey its meaning to the other members of the group by any method he could think of except by speaking or writing. Conventional signs of other kinds could not be altogether excluded as no clear line can be drawn, or at all events explained to children. The agent then proceeded to express by actions, noises, pantomime or drawing, the meaning of the word, and the respondent, as soon as he thought that he understood, would suggest a word. If it was correct the experiment ended, but if it was wrong the experiment went on. As far as possible every action of the agent was recorded as well as the words suggested by the respondents. No hints were given to inform the latter whether their answers were near the mark, but the agent received important guidance from the unsuccessful answers since they showed him how his signs were misconstrued. The same word was given to several groups but not, of course, to different members of the same group. Since different words call for different methods the factor of imitation was in this way reduced to a minimum, while comparison of the methods of different individuals was made possible.

The full details of the experiments are given in the Appendix, but a few of the examples are recorded in the following table, where they are placed alongside examples illustrating the methods used for conveying the same ideas in the deaf and dumb institution in Berlin and in the gesture-languages of the North American Indians and the Cistercian monks. My information concerning these is taken from Tylor's *The Early History of Mankind,* whence also the quotations in the table derive. Tylor emphasizes that all the gestures tend to be accompanied by facial expressions where these can give any assistance.

	The boy acting as agent	Deaf and Dumb (DD) Indians (I) Cistercians (C)
hear	Puts hand to his ear and listens (this understood as 'deaf'), beats imaginary drum and listens with hand round his ear.	(DD) touch ear with forefinger.
house	Makes imaginary tiny walls on ground with hands as if out of mud, indicates doors and windows with fingers.	(DD) draw air-outline of roof and walls. (C) make a roof with fingers.
meat	Carves and eats, points to his own skin, points downstairs (i.e. to dining-room and kitchen), draws plate on table. Munches. Cuts imaginary piece off cheek.	(DD) pull up pinch of flesh from back of hand.
good	Corrects imaginary exercise, claps hands, holds sheet of paper to represent the exercise. Pretends to eat something, smiles with pleasure.	(DD) show thumb. (I) wave hand from mouth, extending thumb from index, and closing the other three fingers. Or, wave hand back upwards in horizontal curve outwards ('gesture of benediction').
fire	Points to gas-stove. Imaginary shovelling. Warms his hands. Or, points to gas-fire. Puts books together on ground as if making a fire.	(I) blow it and warm hands at it. Or, imitate flames with fingers. (C) hold up forefinger and blow out like candle.
river	Pretends to fish with line. Swimming action. Indicates course on ground. Or, pretends to dig narrow trench and pour water in out of can.	(I) perform action of scooping with hand and then drinking, followed by action of waving hands with palms downwards 'to denote an extended surface'.

It will be seen that the methods employed by the boys differ from the others chiefly in being improvised instead of being fixed and conventional. The signs were often quite elaborate and would rather be called pantomime than gesture. For example, to represent a ship one boy went through the performance of stepping into a boat, hoisting sail, taking the tiller in his hand, and in general suggesting by his attitude and movements that he was really in a boat. The gesture-language described by Tylor involves nothing of this kind, and it is clear that for the practical needs of communication such methods would be intolerably slow and inconvenient. On the other hand the brief and economical gestures of the deaf and dumb, of the American Indians, and of the silent monks depended on the establishment of numerous conventions which could only be the result of time. In another series of experiments, not here recorded, a single small group of boys worked together for several weeks in the construction of a language. During the daily sessions they were under the same restrictions as in the experiments I have described. Instead of words they were given sentences to convey and in the first place they had to do so by means of pantomime and gesture. But whenever they succeeded in making clear a particular idea they invented a word which was duly recorded and which they might thereafter use in any future explanation. In this way a considerable vocabulary was formed, and it was observable that in the course of this more protracted intercourse the gestures which continued to be necessary tended to become abridged and stylized. In the first series of experiments this process was scarcely possible since each group was only in action for a comparatively short time. The abbreviation and consequent conventionalization of signs is the result of practice and depends on the continual co-operation of members of a single community.

We may classify the methods employed by these boys in two ways, either according to the nature of the action, as drawing, acting, grimacing, etc., or according to the relation between action and meaning. Classification in the former way yields the following principal categories:

Demonstrative: Holding up the object in the hand, or pointing to it, or looking towards it.

Dramatic: Performing some action, with or without stage effects, or imitating the movements of an animal.

Manual Dramatic: Movement of the hand or fingers to represent an action.

Manual Plastic: Manipulation of the hands to imitate the shape of an object.

Plastic: Construction of model out of handy objects and materials.

Aerial Plastic: Modelling with the hands in the air.

Drawing: Either visibly on paper or with the finger on the ground or in the air.

Facial Expression.

Vocal Sounds.

The last were little used, but the generally prevailing silence was perhaps due to the fact that speech impulses had to be continually suppressed and by extension other vocal expressions were inhibited. If we suppose that there was a time when men were limited to such methods as these, we certainly may not assume that they made no better use of their voices.

With regard to the relation between action and meaning we note that it may be more or less direct. To express the idea of rain one boy went through the action of putting up an imaginary umbrella. In such a case the visible sign consists merely in a particular movement of hands and arms which suggests the handling of a familiar article. Yet it is neither the movement nor the umbrella which he was trying to express, but the rain, that is to say, the imaginary reason for putting up the imaginary umbrella.

The material resources available to the boys in these experiments were restricted. Not very many of the words could be indicated by simple presentation or pointing, and chairs, newspapers, paper-knives and walking-sticks did not provide much material for construction. But it is probable that full use would have been made of any objects that were accessible. The boys would often look round for something to aid their demonstration. We may therefore assume, although the record does not include any very definite examples, that an object would naturally be used to suggest an action as readily as an action to suggest an object.

Thus action and object which are naturally associated may be used to suggest one another, and that which is suggested may itself only serve to suggest something else. In all these cases the respondent must, of course, be familiar with the actions and the objects and with their normal relations to one another. But there is another kind of association which does not depend on such knowledge. The action performed or the object presented may be merely imitations. A movement of the arms suggests the wings of a bird, crawling on all fours suggests the action of a quadruped, a stick suggests a sword or a fishing-rod, a chair suggests a boat. If the imitation is close it may suffice, but if it is crude it must be supplemented with a suggestive action.

In most cases the unavoidable ambiguity can be overcome only by the multiplication of signs. If the correct meaning is divined at once, this may be mere good luck, not because the signs are unambiguous. The more abstract ideas, like *colour, empty, wet* are essentially more difficult to convey. The signs which must be used all tend to suggest at first concrete objects or actions, and it is only by a sequence of different signs, representing different concrete objects or actions, that attention can be called to a common quality. To suggest *colour* one boy pointed to a red book. This was interpreted as *book* and then *red*, and there are, of course, many other possible associated ideas. Since all objects have some colour it is obviously difficult to select such as shall compel the respondent to make the correct abstraction. If the abstract idea of 'colour' had not already existed in his mind, firmly established in relation to a familiar English word, it would no doubt have been impossible to convey the idea.

In view of the large element of convention in many if not most of the deaf and dumb and other signs recorded by Tylor, it seems strange to find him claiming that they are all 'natural', by which he means that the relation between idea and sign is always clear. But although there may exist a relation between the idea and the sign, and although this may be evident, it does not follow that the meaning of the sign can at once be recognized. An example he mentions is the Indians' sign for 'brother' or 'sister', which consists in putting the forefingers of both hands into the mouth 'to show that both fed from the same breast'. Now however eloquent this gesture may be once understood, it certainly does not carry its meaning in itself. Tylor explains that it is a special adaptation of the sign for 'likeness', which consists in showing the two forefingers together and, he says, 'is understood everywhere'. Doubtless it is a common sign in the current gesture-language, but it could suggest at least three ideas—those of finger, of two, and of likeness, apart from what might also be suggested by the manner in which the fingers were presented. In order to single out the one meaning which is intended, it would be necessary to make at least one more sign. It would be easy to eliminate the 'finger', by showing two eyes or two feet, but this would not eliminate the 'two'. In actual practice, of course, it will be found that signs, which once accepted are readily understood, may be far from intelligible in improvisation.

In what then does naturalness consist? In what way do such gestures differ from what Tylor would understand by a purely arbitrary sign? And why do so many of the signs used by the deaf and dumb, and others who make habitual use of gesture-language, belong to this category? The answer surely is that some signs are more easily remembered, and that any kind of association between the sign and the meaning aids the memory and so favours the survival of such signs. This is one of the most important factors in all kinds of language. Where the memory is concerned, associations are essential. Mere habit will, in time, establish an association between any sign and any meaning, but where there are many signs to be remembered, and where alternatives are available, there will, in any established community, tend to be a selection of the fittest. And among other factors, easy retention will be one of the most important. This is, no doubt, the reason why there are many onomatopoeic words in all languages, and why there is sound-symbolism and metaphor. Such words are not invented because they sound like what they mean, they merely survive because they are easy to remember.

If the signs of the gesture-languages are mostly 'natural' in this sense, whereas the words of oral languages are only occasionally so, the explanation must be that in gesture it is much easier to represent directly shapes and movements; that the total vocabulary in the gesture-languages is small compared with any oral language; and that the memory for words has been for so long specially cultivated. There can be no doubt that the human brain has become organized for speech. Finally, the brevity and speed of oral language makes another resource available, namely that of composition, which I shall discuss later.

Wundt notes, in his account of gesture-languages which are or have been in use, that the sign for 'water' may be the hand hollowed in the shape of a drinking vessel, the action of drinking, or the extension of hand or arm in the direction of real water. This variety is not surprising, for the need to express the idea of water may arise in many entirely different circumstances. Perhaps a drink is required, or a swim; perhaps somebody has been drowned or his house flooded. Perhaps it is only that the flowers need water, or there is some cement to be mixed. In each case the idea in the mind of the agent will involve and include water merely as a component in a more complex situation, and in order to convey his idea as a whole he must select those elements which seem most important or most easily portrayed. If, then, he has chosen 'water' for either of these reasons, he must find a means of representing it. Since it may be associated in his mind with *all* these situations he may suggest it by an action which indicates any one of them. He may use a gesture to depict drinking, swimming, drowning, and so on. If he wants to drink he will probably choose the first, and if he wants to swim the second. Since it is hardly likely that he will want to express the isolated idea of water, divorced from any particular context, the sign which is used will almost certainly include more than that abstracted idea. Consequently where more than one method exists for the expression of a particular idea, that method is likely to be chosen which includes as much as possible of the context. We are accustomed to analyse our environment into *things* in accordance with our stock of words. But where communication has not been reduced entirely to a system of conventional signs, whether oral or gestural, there will be some improvisation, and signs employed may be more or less comprehensive according to circumstances. The sentence 'he has cut his finger with a knife' seems to be composed of four distinct ideas, he, cut, finger, knife. And one might suppose perhaps that in gesture-language it would be necessary to use four signs, together with some additional sign to indicate the relation between these main ideas, the relation which in oral language is suggested by prepositions, auxiliaries, etc. But a single gesture, in which two fingers of the right hand, representing the knife, are made to slide across the forefinger of the left hand, followed by a facial expression and movement of the left hand to the lips, conveys the last three ideas together with their relation, and a pointing gesture provides the 'he'. It would be a somewhat artificial analysis of such a gestural communication to say that the two fingers of the right hand denote 'knife', the movement 'cut', and the forefinger of the left hand 'finger', since these separate components would have little or no meaning (except by convention) apart from the context.

Tylor notes that the conventional gesture-language has what one might call syntax; that the usual construction of the deaf-mutes is not 'black horse' but 'horse black'; not 'bring a black hat', but 'hat black bring'; not 'I am hungry give me bread' but 'hungry me bread give'. The order of the signs is determined by the relative importance, in the communication, of the constituent ideas. Thus it is normal for the sign for the action to precede that for the actor. To say 'The carpenter struck me on the arm', the deaf-mute will strike himself on the arm, and then make the sign of planing, as if to say 'I was struck on the arm, the planing-man did it'.

It is of interest to see how the conventional gesture-languages express more difficult notions such as causation. Tylor says that the deaf and dumb man would express e.g. the statement that a man died of drinking by saying he died, 'drank, drank, drank'; and that if the inquiry were made 'died, did he?' he could put the causation beyond doubt by answering, 'yes he drank, drank, and drank'. The connexion must, of course, be understood by the hearer, and so it would be more difficult, perhaps, to explain that a man died of laughing or of sheer joy.

In his discussion of the methods adopted to express abstract ideas, Tylor says:

To 'make' is too abstract an idea for the deaf-mute; to show that the tailor makes the coat or that the carpenter makes the table, he would represent the tailor sewing the coat, and the carpenter sawing and planing the table. Such a proposition as 'Rain makes the land fruitful' would not come into his way of thinking; 'rain falls, plants grow' would be his pictorial expression.

Here again we see that a sign for the particular must replace the sign for the general. But there are two points here of greater importance. First, Tylor has confused words with ideas: the word 'make' in such sentences does not express a general idea but is merely an easy substitute for the correct word. There may be some general notion common to the relation between carpenter and table and that between rain and crops, but if so it is probably derived from the suggestion of language and not from a comparison of the phenomena themselves. It is only if the word 'make' were used in a context which required that it should stand for *all* the different kinds of 'making', that we should be justified in speaking of a general idea. Such words as 'do' and 'have' *may* be used in a general sense, though seldom usefully, but as a rule they are merely general-purpose words, carelessly used in cases where the meaning is sufficiently obvious not to call for any precise terminology. In the second place, where really general words are required it is more difficult, and often impossible, to express them by signs which have any congruity with their meaning. One may represent the operations of sewing, sawing, digging, brick-laying, and so on, but no sign could be devised that would represent all these at the same time. Only a purely conventional sign can do this. Hence, in the absence of conventional signs, a sample selection must be offered from representable particulars to suggest the general idea.

There is one principle that we may everywhere take for granted, namely that the methods of expression are adapted to the circumstances. What is easily understood in one situation may be unintelligible in another. 'Dog, Peter' may mean 'Peter's dog' or 'the dog, Peter', and without context or common knowledge between speaker and hearer there would be nothing to distinguish. But in the presence of an intelligible context there would be no need to do so. We shall see later that this principle plays a more important part in oral language than is sometimes realized.

CHAPTER 7

Pictorial and Plastic Representation

In the experiments described in Chapter 6, the boys resorted to various methods of representing objects, such as modelling with the hands and drawing. These methods, though less conventionalized than those of the deaf and dumb, cannot be regarded as entirely 'natural'. The boys were already used to the idea of picture-stories, and there is a good deal of convention involved in all two-dimensional representations. If we are to suppose that communication by means of speech was preceded by a gesture-language, we have to ask how the representative elements in gesture-language could have arisen.

It is clear that imitation of objects by plastic and pictorial methods is beyond the capacity of any animal other than man. Thus we have to inquire how this human capacity for representation could conceivably arise, and whether pictorial and plastic methods were developed for some other purpose before they were exploited for the purpose of communication.

Wundt, in his *Völkerpsychologie* (Vol. 1, pp.240ff), discusses picture-writing, and has a good deal to say about the probable development of representative art once it had been discovered; but for an explanation of its origins he is driven to the assumption of a natural tendency in primitive man to imitate his experiences either by gesture or by drawing. But since no other animal shows such a tendency, the biologist who believes in human evolution has here something to explain. Given the practice of representing objects or events by models or drawings, we can understand that circumstances would easily arise which led to the discovery of their use as a means of communication. As with all inventions, at least in the primitive stage, the effect would chance to occur and be observed before it could be deliberately aimed at. But as for the practice of drawing itself, Wundt can only assure us that it is a natural impulse.

If we are to trace the human activities of model-making and drawing to activities which we share with other animals, there are two which deserve consideration, namely *curiosity* and *play*. Animals have their attention attracted by unusual shapes and movements, sounds and smells, even when these are quite novel and can suggest no particular utility and no particular danger. Pavlov found his experiments continually affected by what he called the 'investigatory reflex'. The unfamiliar is potentially dangerous, and reassurance is dependent on some kind of explanation. As to the second, all mammals, probably, are given to play. By this I mean that they will at times perform complex actions for no apparent purpose but for the pleasure of the action itself. In times of stress the animal must attend to business; but there are times when he may relax, when he is nevertheless not inclined to sleep, his vital energies prompting him to activity. At such times he can only perform the various items of his normal repertoire, and so play activities often copy business activities. Newly-acquired forms of behaviour are often exploited in play, but in the course of its play an animal may learn new adaptations of behaviour.

The first of these tendencies — the investigation of unfamiliar objects or events — may be supposed to occur when an unusually-shaped object is encountered; for instance a stone bearing a rough likeness to an animal's head, or a root resembling a man's trunk and legs. There is, in fact, archaeological evidence that such objects were formerly collected and preserved (as they often are today). Flinders Petrie found in a prehistoric Egyptian temple, along with ape figurines of ivory and terra cotta, an unworked flint nodule, which appeared to him to have been saved because of its likeness to a baboon. MacCurdy speaks of the finding, in palaeolithic gravel beds, of a flint nodule resembling a bird's head, with the nodular crust intact except for a little chip taken out exactly where the eye should be. He states that there are numerous known examples from later periods of similar retouching of nature's handiwork.

Now, assuming that the finder of such a figure stone had a use for it, and assuming further that the stone was the more useful to him the more accurately it represented the real object, then we can understand how men might have learned to complete or improve a likeness which nature had only suggested. We can understand also how the practice of touching up figures would lead to increasing skill, and how the additions and improvements would become more extensive, until it might be possible to make a good figure out of a very rough stone. The whole process differs in no way, technically, from that of shaping a flint scraper or other tool. But whereas the use of the tool seems quite obvious, and we can understand how need and opportunity might lead to the invention, in the case of the bird-like stone we seem to be unable to suggest any motive for the interest or any use for the product. The question is, why did men take an interest in such stones, what did they do with them, how did they regard them? Part of the answer, I suggest, lies in the investigatory response to the unfamiliar, which we share with other animals. The surprising finding of a stone in the shape of a bird's head calls for an explanation; and curiosity and anxiety are not allayed until an explanation is found. It seems to be in relation to this state of mind that man's interest in fetish objects was developed. Under the influence of fear and curiosity fantastic beliefs easily arose.

As well as three-dimensional 'models' in the form of stones, sticks, or roots, nature can provide examples of representation in two dimensions. Discoloured rock surfaces, the tracings of leaf-mining insects, scarified tree-trunks, may suggest the outline of a familiar object. Such natural outlines, like natural models, lend themselves to retouching. An indication of this process, though from a later period than the one which concerns us, can be seen in the roof paintings in the Altamira caves, where a natural boss on the rock face has been converted by touches of pigment into the representation of a hunched-up bison.

The retouching of naturally occurring shapes, to enhance their resemblance to animals or men, may be regarded as a form of play. Small children may discover the properties of a pencil or a charred stick, and proceed to cover the walls of a room with random scribblings. It is said that a chimpanzee, given a paint brush and a pot of paint, needs little encouragement to use them in a similar fashion. From time to time, the results of such random scribbling will bear a fortuitous likeness to some known object; the step taken by the scribbler when he observes such a likeness and deliberately adds a few enhancing touches, does not seem to be an inconceivably long one. Once it is taken, all that is needed for repetition, practice, and extension of the performance is the scribbler's pleasure in his achievements and the admiration of his fellows.

The two-dimensional representation of a solid object is something so familiar to us today that we are apt to overlook the element of convention that it involves. In general, a drawing or painting represents a solid object as seen from one particular point of view; but our *idea* of the object is a composite one. Children and untaught people have difficulties in drawing and are apt to put incompatible elements into their pictures. More sophisticated artists (for instance, in ancient Egypt) have evolved conventions by which the parts of the human body, for example, are represented in their most typical or interesting aspects, even though these aspects are never simultaneously visible in the real object. The most striking and the most complete aspect of a quadruped is its profile; the human head is also most striking (and easiest to represent on a plane surface) in profile, but the body is seen most completely and characteristically from the front. Accordingly we find that in the Egyptian hieroglyphs the numerous human figures have, as a rule, the head in profile, while the bust may be partly turned to the front so as to show the two arms. Mammals and birds are nearly all shown in side view. The Sacred Beetle, the lizard, the scorpion and the turtle are, understandably, shown from the dorsal aspect. All the paintings reproduced in Maspero's *Art in Egypt* show the face in profile, whether the remainder of the body is in profile or not.

The ability to reproduce faithfully a single, remembered aspect of a thing seen appears to depend on a highly variable inborn faculty, to which Galton first drew attention, and which has been called the 'eidetic' faculty: an ability, that is, to retain in the memory a vivid two-dimensional picture of the thing seen, undistorted by memories of other aspects of the thing. To what extent a faculty of this kind is shared by other animals is not known.

However men first learned to make images or pictures, there is every reason to suppose that those who were skilful at the work would pursue it not only for business purposes, whatever these might be, but also in play, that is, for its own sake. There is no lack of evidence that even such things of real utility as knives, axes, spears and shields were often made for the pleasure of the work, refinements and decorations being added which have no relation to the function of the weapons or may even, in some cases, make them useless. But sometimes a development of this kind, which we may suppose to have arisen out of the craftsman's pleasure in his work, may come to have a new use and be the foundation of a new business activity. Hence, in seeking the antecedents of any particular form of activity we have to take into account two possibilities: there may have been a development of some business activity into a play activity, or vice versa. The latter may easily be illustrated from the history of human inventions.

If then the craftsman, fashioning weapons or other useful objects, is led by his creative satisfaction and consciousness of skill to refine on the requirements of pure utility, and if he allows himself to be led by the hints offered by the materials in which he works, he may find himself converting practical shapes into artistic imitations. It would be in the fashioning of instruments of wood and bone that such suggestions and possibilities would most easily arise.

As we have seen, models may be used for the purpose of communication. Given the practice of making models we can understand how it might be adapted for that purpose. But can we suppose that the need for communication would of itself lead to the making of models? We can hardly suppose that models would be made by accident during an endeavour to communicate by gestures. But, as we have seen, gestural communication in its primitive form involves the use of objects of various kinds, and in the absence of the real article dummies are made use of. At first such dummies might bear no more resemblance to the object they represent than is necessary for the handling, since the nature of the article is indicated by the action. But if misunderstanding arises from the ambiguity of the dummy a small improvement may be made to correct the error. And here would at once be supplied the motive for correction and an external control to guide it. The dummy would be altered until communication was achieved. A story told by Herodotus illustrates the use of real objects in messages. When Darius was seeking to bring the Scythians to bay, the latter dispatched to him a herald bearing gifts in the shape of a bird, a mouse, a frog and five arrows. The animals were apparently real, and it was taken for granted by Darius that they were intended to convey a message. What it was could only be conjectured, and more than one interpretation was proposed. Here of course some kind of symbolism was involved. But in more primitive times we may suppose that messages were conveyed in a similar way, and that as between persons who understood one another and were accustomed to the mode of communication they would be more readily interpreted. If now for this purpose substitutes were sometimes used there would be a further opportunity for practice in the making of copies and models.

It must be remembered that in all manufacturing efforts except those of the pioneer, there is always an element of imitation. The knife or axe is made according to a model, and one arrow must be exactly like the other. Such copying work trains the eye and brain to reproduce shapes of all kinds. In resorting to the principle of imitation to explain behaviour of any kind we have to be cautious, as we have already seen. But I am now assuming that the practice had been established in relation to the making of tools before it was transferred to the carving of images. But the workman who could shape a stone or a piece of wood in imitation of one kind of model might learn to copy another.

Finally, drawing that was not representative could have been developed for the purpose of giving names to individuals. Although one rabbit is, for most purposes, the same as another, in the case of our human companions differences are almost more important than resemblances, and so we find it necessary to give each individual a separate name. But the provision of such proper names presents a special problem. Descriptive signs are, in general, unsuitable, and this is particularly evident in the case of pictures. For although a man may easily be represented by a very rude outline, it is a much more difficult thing to represent the peculiarities of the individual. Arbitrary signs, or signs suggested by various associations, must therefore replace directly representative signs. The marks of ownership or trademarks can obviously not be representative and must be conventional. They may, of course, consist in drawings which represent real objects, birds, lizards, etc, but such objects do not constitute the meanings of the signs. On the other hand the trademark may be some non-representative sign like a cross or a circle, or any other meaningless mark. And it is quite possible that marks which revealed the identity of the manufacturer were at first unintentional. The author of an unsigned work may sometimes be known from internal evidence. The mark of the artist may consist in some peculiarity in the work itself. The discovery that such marks have an interest or a utility, especially if they prove useful to the artist, will lead to their deliberate employment. These considerations serve to show that there are other possible sources for pictography than representative drawing.

None of these suggestions is entirely satisfactory by itself, but taken together they seem to make the beginnings of plastic representation partially intelligible. In any case the problem is not to be avoided. The raw materials out of which gesture and speech were formed were already available in the behaviour of the ape. In these cases, therefore, we have only to explain how the existing behaviour became adapted. But the raw material of pictorial language is not to be found even in the most rudimentary form in the behaviour of any mammal, so that here we have a second problem to solve.

It seems necessary to assume that some kind of communication already existed before models could be employed for the purpose. It is true that the palaeolithic drawings and sculptures are older than any records of language. But since gesture and speech can leave no independent record of themselves, we cannot infer from this that pictorial language is older than any other.

Perhaps we can best summarize the results of the foregoing discussion by saying that just as gesture is derived from executive acts reduced and modified for the special purpose of communication, so models and pictures are derived from the real objects or dummies which were employed in conjunction with gestures. As the gesture is a simulated act, so the model or picture is a simulated object. The earliest form of communication must have consisted in real acts with real objects. But as the nature and needs of communication gradually came to be understood, both act and object were replaced by readier substitutes in which only those properties were retained which were found to be indispensable for this purpose. In the one case the transformation can be explained by the general principles which I have described under the names of streamlining, stylization, standardization, etc., but in the other the process was evidently more complex.

CHAPTER 8

Writing

Writing as we now know it is, of course, a system of signs representing not ideas or things but sounds, and but for an already existing connexion between sound and meaning such writing would be impossible. Picture-writing on the other hand need owe nothing to speech, and there is therefore no reason why it should not have existed in a primitive form before any other kind of descriptive language. No doubt pictures were used in conjunction with other methods of communication, as they still are and probably always will be. They would only require to be used alone for the purpose of sending messages or leaving records. But for these purposes their scope was limited. The hieroglyphic writing in Egypt, the cuneiform writing of Babylonia and Assyria, and Chinese writing, are all largely dependent on oral language and as far back as they can be traced in history no stage is known where this is not true. But although, for example, many Egyptian characters which represent objects are used phonetically and do not by any means always convey what they seem most evidently to suggest, yet we may presume that they were originally used to convey the idea of the object they depict. How they later came to be used phonetically is intelligible enough. The important step consists in the use of a picture to represent, not the object it resembles, but the sound which in the oral language happens to denote that object and so, indirectly, every other object or idea denoted by the same sound. It is as though the sign for 'the sea' were used also to represent the idea 'to see' and, in combination with some other sign for the remaining sound, the ideas 'season', 'secret', 'seal', and so on. Ambiguities may be removed by the addition of a pictograph representing a related idea. The sounds thus represented may be complex or simple. In due course the spoken language is analysed into a comparatively small number of sounds, so that a not too great number of signs suffices for the representation of the whole vocabulary. The final stage of the process was the alphabet. But even when, as in Egypt, an alphabet existed, it was long before it was relied on alone. The hieroglyphics are a mixture of pictographs, syllabics and alphabetic signs. The cuneiform writing is essentially syllabic, and the Chinese system is also mixed. Thus none of these systems of writing afford an illustration of pure pictographic writing.

These developments have little bearing on the origin and nature of communication. It is the possibility of using pictographs independently of oral language that we must study here. Now the word 'pictograph' suggests a recognizable picture of some animal or object, and the Egyptian hieroglyphs are to a large extent composed of such pictures. They tend to become conventionalized and cease to be recognizable representations of anything, but this change does not of itself involve any dependence on oral language. If a picture-language were possible there is no reason why the pictures should not be replaced by conventional signs. We must therefore keep distinct two processes, on the one hand the gradual conventionalization of signs by which they lose their representative virtue, and on the other the gradual transfer of signs from things or ideas to sounds.

Let us now consider the Egyptian characters on the assumption that they were originally used in their obvious sense. Many of them are direct representations of objects. They are, of course, standardized, and in rapid writing tend to be streamlined. Nevertheless, the following examples (taken from Budge, 1922) are obviously representative characters:

Now concrete objects with a constant and familiar shape do not comprise the whole range of important topics of communication, and so indirect representation must evidently play an important part. It is interesting to note, as was long ago pointed out by Warburton, that the Egyptian writers were able to borrow hints from the gesture-language. The following hieroglyphs illustrate this device, and it will be seen that they are only a little less intelligible than those which directly represent concrete objects.

It is naturally chiefly human gestures that are exploited in this way, but there are some characters in which the movements of animals are represented. The meanings of the following hieroglyphs are 'to find', 'to hunt', 'to fly' and 'to alight' or 'hover'.

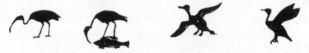

Any kind of association between sign and meaning may be utilized in sign symbolism, and it would be useless to try and draw up an exhaustive list of categories. It may be well, however, to note some of the more important, since they recur of necessity in every form of communication and are as indispensable today in the descriptive language of science as they were when the art of communication was still young.

Materials may be represented by pictures of objects which are typically composed of them. Thus wood is denoted by the picture of a tree-branch and leather or skin by a piece of animal's hide. Qualities are represented by pictures of animals or objects which are, or are supposed to be, characterized by them. Thus the jackal, the sparrow, the turtle, the lizard (or tadpole?), and the young plant denote respectively 'wise', 'little', 'evil', 'abundant' and 'green'. Combinations of signs serve to express a more complex idea, as the arrow piercing an animal's skin means 'to hunt', the conjunction of flesh and bone means 'progeny', that of water and sky 'rain' (see below, p. 71). Horns are the sign for the 'beginning' or the 'fore-part', and a young plant shoot for the renewal of vegetation, and in combination they signify the new year. 'To go in' and 'to go 'out' are represented by an asp in relation to its hole, either entering or emerging.

In the old Sumerian picture-writing a bowl under a mouth expressed the idea of eating, and in early Chinese pictographs 'father' was denoted by a hand grasping a stick.

We are inclined now to make a distinction between the ideas expressed by different parts of speech, as 'die', 'dead', 'death', and 'deadly'. But when we try to represent any of these ideas by means of a picture we find that almost any sign we may use will suggest equally easily any one of them, the choice depending solely on the relation in which the idea stands to other ideas in the same communication. Thus we find in Egyptian writing the same sign used indifferently for verb, noun or adjective. The sign which represents water being poured out of a jar denotes 'pure', 'purify' or 'purification'. If combined with the figure of a man it denotes 'priest'. The scarab means 'to come into being', to 'create', 'the creature' and 'the creator'. The duck (?) means to 'go in' and also 'one who enters'. The adaptability of signs depends, of course, on their ambiguity. If a sign could only denote one specific idea, it could not be used to suggest another. But ideas cannot be isolated, and it is seldom possible to evoke one idea in a person's mind without a train of others which are related to it. Wherever pictures or gestures are used this variety of meanings is inevitable, for the *natural* meaning of a thing, as we have seen, is always complex and includes everything that the observer may be made to think of. Since, then, the sign must necessarily be variously interpreted according to circumstances, it is natural that the agent, observing this, should take advantage of it for his purposes.

To avoid this ambiguity the only real resource is the multiplication of signs. This, as I have previously shown, may consist in setting side by side two or more alternative signs for the same notion, so that the alternative meanings which do not coincide may be eliminated. Or it may simply consist in the construction of phrases or sentences in which the individual signs, from the known relations between the things they represent, limit each other's meaning. The latter process of mutual elucidation occurs in every connected sequence of signs where the latter have a real relation to objective facts. It fails only where the signs are devoid of such relation. The subject will be further illustrated in a later chapter in connexion with oral language.

The combination of pictographs which have a common meaning could no doubt be illustrated from Egyptian hieroglyphic writing. But far more common in fact appears to be another kind of duplication, that namely which consists in setting phonetic symbols alongside the pictographs. And the phonetic symbols themselves are sometimes duplicated, syllabics and alphabetics being used side by side.

Many ambiguities are gradually eliminated by conventionalization. The less suggestive a sign is in its own nature the easier it is to restrict its meaning. The ancient Chinese character for to 'stand' was . It was simplified in various ways and eventually ended in the conventional form . Similarly the old form for 'to shoot' was . This passed through the intermediate form to . The recognizable picture has a power of suggestion in itself that cannot be excluded altogether by any convention; and so whatever the user of the sign may intend to convey, it is likely that much else will be suggested in addition. But the purely conventional sign which has lost all recognizable relation to any known object has also lost all its 'natural' significance and can therefore convey nothing that has not been in some way embodied in it by convention and use. It does not, of course, follow that its meaning must be precise and unambiguous, but at least much irrelevant suggestiveness has been excluded.

As against this advantage of the conventional sign we must recognize that it is generally less easy to remember. We may suppose that at first any tendency to abridge and disguise the characters would be resisted by the need to avoid confusion due to the loss of intelligibility, and it is improbable that at any time any systematic conventionalization took place with the conscious aim of obtaining less ambiguous signs. Conventionalization, like nearly every other phase in the development of human communication, came about unconsciously as the result of certain general tendencies. I do not mean that there was no deliberate choice or conscious effort to adapt means to ends, but such efforts were concerned with immediate needs and were not guided by a long view. The benefits of a particular procedure were not foreseen, they were discovered. But when they were once recognized they were exploited to the full. At first, then, the simplification of signs did not disguise their original form but merely reduced the labour of writing. The hieratic script carried the process further and most of the characters seem to have been completely disguised. Although it may be possible to see the ghost of the hieroglyphic original if one knows what it is, the hieratic form is itself certainly not, in most cases, a recognizable representation of any natural object.

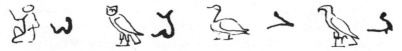

Such forms were no doubt only introduced gradually and they retained their intelligibility partly because of the easy transition from one phase to another through intermediate stages, and partly because of the continual influence of mutual elucidation — that is to say, the explanatory virtue of a context. The Egyptian characters illustrate well the process of streamlining, but not so clearly that of stylization, as defined earlier in Chapter 5. This process, or at least its final effect, is much more evident in the cuneiform and Chinese writing. The transition forms are not, of course, always preserved. Barton gives a large number of Babylonian or Sumerian pictographs with their cuneiform equivalents. To the uninitiated the connexion between the two often seems obscure, but the two ends of the process are evident enough. Compared with the Egyptian pictographs the characters are crude indeed, and the early conventionalization is generally attributed to the method of writing. Instead of using a stylus or brush to apply ink to a hard surface, the Babylonians impressed their characters on clay with a kind of spatula. This method restricted them to the use of straight lines, and excluded also the use of continuous lines, since the instrument was used to make a series of similar impressions. This gives an air of conventionalization even to the obvious pictographs. I copy below some of Barton's figures with his explanations.

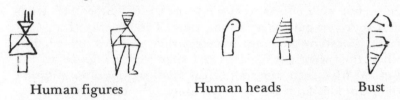

Human figures   Human heads   Bust

The cuneiform equivalents of the first two of these characters

are ⊣|||⟨ |||⊒⏋ and ⊢⊣ ⟍⟍|| . Whether or not we suppose

the latter to be directly derived from the former it is certain that these typical cuneiform words have evolved from pictographs. That does not mean that every cuneiform word or character must have a pictograph original. A picture may be reduced at first to straight lines of many different lengths and fairly numerous. Standardization will simplify the drawing by reducing their number and variety, and in the end this will give a conventional figure which no longer suggests the original. Its form and the form of its elements will become assimilated to those of other figures and stylization will cause all figures to conform to a certain system or manner. Once this style of writing has been fixed, new characters will be made by composition or differentiation of existing characters. These cannot be traced to pictographic originals since they have none. Now, unless all the intermediate forms survive to reveal the history of a character from its pictographic ancestor, it must remain impossible to say in any given case whether we are dealing with a derived form or a new formation.

All pictographs which represent the same natural object must have a general resemblance to one another wherever they originate. Thus the following signs, in independent pictographic systems, show an unmistakable family likeness.

Water is represented in hieroglyphs by the sign〰, in Sumerian pictograph by〰, and in ancient Chinese by 〻 . In the same three forms of writing mountains are represented by ⏝ , ╱X╲ , and ∿ , respectively. In Egyptian the signs for the sky and for rain are ▭ and ╦╎╎╎ . The modern Chinese character for rain strongly suggests an original of the same kind: 雨

Once the process of stylization begins, these similarities disappear since all signs are assimilated to the local type. The conditions which make for change and those which tend to arrest it are not hard to state in general terms, but it would be a difficult matter to explain the historical sequence in any particular case. They are essentially the same in all forms of communication and may be roughly grouped under four categories — the use to which the mode of communication is put, its relative permanence, the writer, and the reader. Illustrating these with reference only to forms of writing, we may say that there are three principal uses — religious texts, state documents, and private business. Religious texts are generally written and read only by the priests; state documents, royal decrees and records are written only by officials but may be read by a much greater number. Private business writing is carried on by a large section of the population. Religious texts and royal decrees are generally intended to be permanent and are accordingly often written on stone. Private business is often ephemeral. Now the fewer the writers, the slower, in

general, will change be. Changes become rapid when many independent writers are using the same medium. In the religious
texts the conservative forces are strong. Not only is the practice
of writing these texts restricted to a special class, but the very
forms used are regarded as sacrosanct. In all functions of great
social importance we see at work the principle of the special
sanctity of the archaic. However where the ancient formulas
are preserved only by tradition, whether an oral tradition or in
writings that decay and must be copied again and again, there
is a slow erosion. The old forms cease to be intelligible and are
corrupted. But where the ancient writings themselves persist
unaltered through thousands of years, as on many of the
Egyptian monuments, the conservative power of the principle
is reinforced by daily observation.

The general character of a conventional form of writing is
greatly influenced by the medium commonly used. The
Chinese wrote on paper or silk with a brush, the Egyptians on
papyrus with the bruised end of a reed. In both cases the signs
were produced by the application of a coloured ink to a white
or light-coloured surface. But the brush does not lend itself to
a cursive style, and Chinese characters are composed of a
number of separate straight strokes or short dashes, different
only in length and thickness. With a soft-tipped reed on the
other hand one may write almost as with a pen or pencil and
curved continuous characters are easy. The Babylonians, we
saw, used an instrument with which they could make wedge-
shaped impressions in clay, varying only in length.

Where writing was engraved on stone the slowness and the
difficulty of the operation did not lead to abridgment and
streamlining, for such work would not be undertaken except
for a very important purpose and for public display, and its
permanent character would engage the writer to exhibit his
skill. Moreover a cursive script would not be easier to engrave
than any other, while retaining all its own disadvantages. We
should therefore expect to find that stylization and elaboration, rather than streamlining and debasement, resulted from
the practice of writing on stone.

One effect of the establishment of a conventional script is in
a way paralleled in oral language, where Jespersen calls the
phenomenon 'secretion' (1947, p. 384). Those characters

which are merely conventionalized pictures may be complex without being composite. Thus Barton gives the following characters as representing musical instruments:

We must presume that these figures resembled the instruments, or at least the pictographs of the instruments. But there is no reason why, in the first place, such figures should include any recognizable components more complex than the elementary wedges. It is true that there is one group of four wedges which occurs twice in each character, but the more closely the character as a whole corresponds to the original picture the less likely is it that this group of four wedges has any independent significance. However, the formation of a large number of distinct characters from the same elementary wedges would necessarily lead to the occurrence, sooner or later, of recognizable groups of this kind. Thus in Maspero's list of cuneiform syllabics I find the following:

KHIR   ZUK   SHIP   TUS

It is clear that the group of four wedges forming a rectangle is recurrent. Another example is the group of four short wedges: which is found in

BIR   GUN   KHAM

and several others.

Now it does not appear that these common elements of form contribute any common elements of sound or meaning. But a common meaning might come by some chance to be attached to them, and such an accidental correspondence of meaning with form would be encouraged and perhaps extended for its

mnemonic value. The memorizing of such a large number of
characters would be a troublesome task and every aid to the
memory would be encouraged. In Chinese we find the same
prevalence of recurrent elements and it seems at least possible
that in many cases they have resulted in the same way merely
from the limited possibilities of combination. But in Chinese
these distinct components have generally a meaning of their
own, either ideographic or phonetic. The following examples
are taken from Seidel.

酌　配　酒　酸　醉　醋　醒　醜
1.　　2.　　3.　　4.　　5.　　6.　　7.　　8.

The common component 酉 is a sign which has been de-

rived from the pictograph of a jar and meaning *wine* or *to
drink*. And it is not hard to see the connexion between wine
and the meanings of these eight characters, which Seidel gives
as follows: 1. To pour out. 2. Companion. 3. Wine. 4. Sour.
5. Drunk. 6. Vinegar. 7. To become sober. 8. Ugly. It was seen

above that the character meaning 'to shoot' 射 derives from

the pictograph 身寸. The part which would appear to have

represented the hand has come to be a separate character
which enters into the composition of a number of compound
characters whose meanings, however, seem now to have little
in common and nothing in particular to do with the hand or
arm. Here are some given in Seidel's list:

寸　寺　封　射　將　專　尊　對
1.　　2.　　3.　　4.　　5.　　6.　　7.　　8.

Now this appears to me to resemble the phenomenon which
Jespersen has called 'secretion'. A portion of one character is
separated off from the rest arbitrarily and acquires a function
in other combinations which has no relation to its original

meaning. When once the figure has acquired a separate identity in the mind of the scribes any chance association may suggest a meaning for it. The meanings of the above characters appear to be: 1. Inch. 2. Temple. 3. Seal. 4. To Shoot. 5. To Bring. 6. Exclusive. 7. Venerable. 8. To agree. Since the component in question is the class determinant it presumably had some meaning which it contributed at one time. Only a detailed study of the history of these words and signs could settle such points. All that concerns us now, however, is that the components which at present go to make up these composite characters need not have originated from a distinct pictograph. They may have been broken off from a larger character in which they were an appendage of no particular significance, any more than the separate strokes of the letter F, which play no distinct part in the representation of the sound.

In order to find an example of relatively pure pictography we have to go to North America. Schoolcraft and Mallery have recorded many examples of the writing of the Indians. But they do not, I think, reveal any new principles beyond what have already been illustrated in the preceding pages, except the manner of combining the separate symbols. In a pure pictographic writing that obtains no assistance from a conventional oral language, the great difficulty is to show the connexion between separate ideas. A sequence of actions or situations can be represented by a series of pictures arranged in the appropriate order. In this way the time relation is indicated. But other relations require less obvious conventional signs. Thus lines are drawn from a man's eyes to the object which he sees, or from his heart to that which causes him emotion. The amount of convention involved in these Indian writings is indicated by the difficulty which uninstructed Europeans have in interpreting them. I give a few examples from Mallery (1886), with his explanations, to illustrate these points. The use made of gestures is as conspicuous here as in the Egyptian hieroglyphs.

1   2   3   4   5

1. The speaker, with the right hand indicating himself, and with the left pointing in the direction to be taken.

2. Holding a boat paddle—going by boat.

3. The right hand to the side of the head, to denote *sleep*, and the left elevated with one finger elevated to signify *one*—one night.

4. The speaker with his harpoon, making the sign of a sea-lion with the left hand. The flat hand is held edgewise with the thumb elevated, then pushed outward from the body in a slightly downward curve.

5. Shooting with bow and arrow.

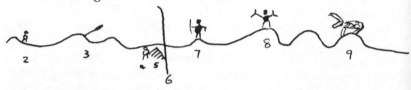

1. Represents the contour lines of the country and mountain peaks.

2. Native going away from home.

3. Stick placed on hill-top, with bunch of grass attached, pointing in the direction he has taken.

4. Native of another settlement, with whom the traveller remained overnight.

5. Lodge.

6. Line representing the end of the first day, i.e., the time between two days; rest.

7. Traveller again on the way.

8. Making signal that on second day (right hand raised with two extended fingers) he saw game (deer, 9) on a hill-top which he secured, so terminating his journey.

The question of the precise origin of these various characters and systems of writing is not, perhaps, of very great importance in itself, although naturally of interest to the archaeologist. But recently strange things have been asserted concerning the relation between signs (or symbols) and the things or ideas which they are used to denote; an extensive literature has grown up about symbolism and semantics and the meaning of meaning from which one might infer that the problem of meaning was beyond the reach of science and could be solved only with the aid of some supernatural inspiration. Yet it is not really so very difficult if one approaches it in a calm spirit, without metaphysical emotion, and bears in mind the simple psychological facts which underlie the relation between signs and the things signified.

To sum the matter up, in the beginning signs must convey their meaning by natural suggestion. But use teaches men to recognize signs when by abridgment and conventionalization they have lost their immediately intelligible form. Later, new signs are invented, not now by the conventionalization of what were once self-explanatory signs, but by the elaboration, differentiation, combination of already existing conventional signs. But however far this process is carried, it remains impossible for man to communicate with his neighbour by means of conventional signs, unless both have first learnt a common set of conventions. And these can be established in the first place only with the aid of natural signs.

CHAPTER 9

The Origin of Oral Language

Oral language is necessarily composed of arbitrary signs; for self-explanatory sounds which can be readily imitated with the voice are far too few to form the basis of the most rudimentary speech. It required the exceptional efficiency of conventional oral language to make it an irresistible rival to the language of movement.

Arbitrary signs grow naturally out of self-explanatory ones by gradual reduction and schematization, and it is not difficult to imagine the origin of the arbitrary signs of the conventional gesture-language, which may be traced back, as we have seen, to dramatic and imitative signs. The difficulty we have in explaining the arbitrary sounds of oral language is that we cannot, except in a very small number of cases, trace them back to any self-explanatory sounds. Once it had been realized that arbitrary sounds could be used as signs, there was no insuperable difficulty in attaching particular meanings to particular sounds. The protests of the nineteenth-century philologists that words never are deliberately invented can hardly be taken seriously in the twentieth, since we now see the process going on every day before our eyes. But how could this realization be brought about? How can we reconcile such a discovery with the principle that every new form of behaviour is adapted from some pre-existing form? To understand this we must first consider what Köhler calls 'insightful' behaviour, which, although not peculiar to man, is much more highly developed in him than in any of his relatives. Köhler used the term 'insight' *(Einsicht)* to mean, roughly, knowing and understanding what one is doing, as against the 'trial and error' behaviour described by Thorndike. A man may learn to perform a certain task, to adapt his actions to certain variations in the conditions, and yet, if he has learnt no more than is strictly necessary for the purpose, we know that he will be helpless as soon as any unusual or unanticipated situation arises. He knows how to handle his machine under normal conditions, but, as he knows nothing of its internal construction, as soon as anything goes wrong he is at a loss. He acts without 'insight' and gets his results without knowing why.

The test for insight is the ability to adapt one's behaviour to unusual variations in the situation, to adopt alternative methods when the accepted ones fail, thus showing that one appreciates the essentials of the problem. Paraffin is a good cleansing agent, and if we do not know why it cleans, we might expect to remove ink-stains with it. A chemist, familiar with reagents of many kinds, knows that the removal of a stain depends on chemical action in one case and physical action in another; but the difference between him and the non-scientist is only a difference in extent of knowledge. If we say that the chemist knows *why* the paraffin is effective this really only means that he knows more precisely *when* it is effective.

Now we must suppose that there was a time when men used signs, knowing quite well what their effects would be but not knowing why they produced those effects—i.e. not knowing when and in what circumstances those effects were to be expected. Magical beliefs have been found all over the world which show that all kinds of powers have been wrongly attributed to language; and to this day philosophers hold views about it which show that they little understand how its effects are produced. But there are many degrees of understanding; and as the precise effect of language became gradually better known and understood, it could be used more intelligently.

Signs are used to elicit certain reactions from the respondent. If they are effective it is for the reasons which I have tried to outline in a previous chapter. But these reasons merely tell us more exactly in what conditions they are effective, and this could be learnt only gradually by those who used them. These conditions include, of course, the nature of the signs used. At first the value and effect of each particular sign must be learnt for itself. At a later stage some degree of generalization occurred and it was realized that those signs were effective which bore some external analogy to the things they repre-

sented or the actions they invited. But this already implies a
considerable degree of abstraction and the practice of experimenting in the imagination. Many signs could be used
which had been learnt by trial and error, and in these cases
there would be no need for any general conception of their
common character. A common character is required only if
new signs are to be invented, that is to say arrived at by a
process of reflexion. It will only be recognized when a large
number of particular signs have already come into use. The
chimpanzee, as we saw, when he is seeking a substitute for a
stick, must carry in his mind a general idea of the kind of object required. With the aid of this general idea he examines
the objects he meets and assesses their properties in relation to
his purpose. So man, looking for means to express his aim,
must have been able to choose a sign in accordance with his
notion of what a sign should be. This notion would be
gradually improved with experience and would supply the
foundation of his understanding of the function and nature of
a sign.

The next stage begins with the reduction, by trial and error,
of a great many signs to an abridged and stylized form. These
abridged signs are no longer effective on strangers, and are
useful only in communication with friends and companions
who have shared in the abbreviating progress. Then at some
time this difference is recognized and the conditions in which
the non-analogical signs can be used are more and more
accurately distinguished. When this has come about it will be
possible to set out deliberately to make such signs available
among the members of a small group, in other words to *invent
a language.*

How long a time would be required to complete such a
process one can only guess. A few individuals would achieve
the new 'insight' long before the majority, but imitation would
ultimately spread the effects. Since no records can possibly
throw any direct light on the matter we can only speculate on
psychological grounds. But the fact that every known human
community, and every one of which we have any record, has
been found to be in possession of a fully developed oral language suggests that once the notion of using arbitrary sounds
for the purpose had been attained, the exploitation of the idea

was rapid. In all languages which have been exhaustively studied and whose history extends over many centuries, it is found that neologisms are rare. New terms, if needed, are usually derived by composition or modification from older ones. It is this fact which has led the philologists to suppose that language cannot have been invented. But we shall see that there is evidence of such invention in certain cases where there was a need for secret languages. Today, of course, invention is made necessary by the enormous and rapid increase of ideas which need a name.

The difference between making a sign and knowing what a sign consists in is given by Tylor as the distinction between human and animal language. He says in his *Anthropology* (p. 123) that a hen can cluck to call her chickens, a bull bellow with rage and toss his head to warn off a dog near his paddock, a dog jump up for food and bark for the door to be opened.

But he adds:

> It is hard to say how far the dog's mind merely associates jumping up with being fed, and barking with being let in, or how far it forms a conception like ours of what it is doing and why it does it .... A dog's mind seems not to go beyond this point, that a good imitation of a mew leads it to look for a cat in the room; whereas a child can soon make out from the nurse saying *miaou* that she means something about some cat, which need not even be near by. That is, a young child can understand what is not proved to have entered the mind of the cleverest dog, elephant, or ape, that a sound may be used as the sign of a thought or idea. Thus, while the lower animals share with man the beginnings of natural language, they hardly get beyond its rudiments, while the human mind easily goes on to higher stages.

One should rather say, perhaps, that the child has a more comprehensive idea of a cat and lives in far more complicated relations with it than a dog. In both dog and child the immediate effect of the sound of the word is to evoke an idea. The comparatively uniform reaction of the dog is due to the fact that there is little else he has learned to do about a cat except to chase it. The young child can hardly be said to understand that sounds may be used as 'signs' for 'ideas', since these notions are much too abstract. But having a more comprehensive idea of a cat the child can imagine it in relation to many different situations besides the actual one, whereas the dog's power of calling up remote and merely possible situations is obviously very limited.

We see then that there are many stages in the process of recognizing what a sign is, how it produces its effect, and how it may best be adapted for that purpose. First there is the recognition that certain acts may be employed simply in order to evoke some desired act from the respondent; second the recognition of certain general characters common to such acts, which permits the improvisation of signs having these characters. Next the practice of communication leads to the abbreviation and stylizing of many of the commonest signs, and this alters the general character of signs, since they are no longer required to suggest their meaning by any kind of analogy or imitation. The important character of these new signs is that they are intelligible only to a limited audience, and the possibility of deliberately inventing such signs depended on the recognition of the nature of convention. The last stage in the process consisted in the recognition of the peculiar aptness of vocal noises for exploitation as conventional signs. And it is with this latest stage that we are now concerned.

The difficulty of understanding this transition from a primitive language of gestures and pantomime to the conventional language of articulate sounds is well illustrated by Sir Richard Paget's theory of 1930. He supposes (pp.132-4) that primitive man's self-explanatory gestures 'were unconsciously copied by movements of the mouth, tongue or lips'; that as man's hands became more occupied with the arts and crafts, they ceased to be available for the performance of gestures, so that the tongue, lips and jaw took over 'the pantomimic art'. Then it was discovered that, if air was blown through the oral cavity while a gesture with the tongue and lips was being made, it became audible. Paget's inadequate proposals could only confirm the view of most of the nineteenth-century philologists, that speech could not derive from gesture at all, and must needs be referred to a natural and unique human impulse.[1] Max Müller, for instance, had seemed quite oblivious of the probable existence of a gesture-language before conventional oral language was available.[2] He wrote:

> No one has yet explained how, without language, a discussion, however imperfect, on the merits of each word, such as must needs have preceded a mutual agreement, could have been carried on. (I,32)

If a language of *visible* signs already existed this difficulty disappears. As a matter of fact Condillac, as long ago as 1746, had anticipated this objection and answered it. He writes (*Oeuvres, I, 362):*

> In order to understand how men agreed together about the meaning of the first words which were introduced, it is enough to observe that they would be uttered in circumstances where everybody would be led to refer them to the same perceptions. In this way they would fix their meaning more precisely according as the circumstances, being repeated, accustomed the mind more and more to attach the same ideas to the same signs. The gesture-language would help to remove ambiguities and uncertainties which, to begin with, would be frequent.

But this is not quite enough. The articulate sounds of which all languages are composed are not the natural sounds by which men express their emotions, but are entirely different from groans and sighs, laughter and cries of fear. We have seen how the various kinds of visible sign could arise from

---

1. Paget's 'mouth-gesture' theory has, however, recently been taken seriously by Hewes, who invokes it in order to explain the 'initial stages' of the transition from gestural to vocal language. Hewes, like other writers who have argued for the gestural origin of language, finds this transition very difficult to explain, and deems it necessary to posit (p.xiii) 'an evolutionary neutral transformation' (Eds.).

2. Swadesh also discusses gesture (pp.162ff) but seems to regard it simply as an interesting alternative method of communication. He also (p.179) considers it to be 'formal' or 'artificial' (i.e. dependent on conventions), doubtless because he has in mind the gesture-languages of the deaf and dumb in use in modern society. He does, however, very properly distinguish between two 'levels' of communication — (1) the instinctive-intuitive and (2) the formal-conventional or arbitrary; and he says too that 'the formal systems of communication must have crystallized out of the intuitive' (Eds.).

natural actions of another kind. But how could the modulations of voice used in language be derived from any instinctive or natural noises? Lord Monboddo, writing a generation after Condillac, was fully conscious of this difficulty. In the first place, he said, man does not naturally form articulate sounds, and therefore this use of the vocal apparatus had to be discovered and practised before it was available. And even when a supply of serviceable syllables had been provided by some intelligent prevision or fortunate chance, it was far from obvious how they could be employed for the expression of ideas, 'with the greater part of which they have no connexion' (I, 460). He solves the problem by resort to the principle of imitation, and supposes that men learned to produce the articulate sounds required for speech by imitating the cries of animals and songs of birds. It is not, of course, a question of onomatopoeia. The problem first was to obtain the vocal materials, not to make signs. Whether there is a *fundamental* difference, as Monboddo thought, between articulate and inarticulate sounds, we may doubt, and may say rather that the real difference is merely a matter of voluntary control, the acquisition of which need constitute no more mystery than that of control over the fingers. The ape can use his fingers for clasping, poking, scratching, and so on, and these movements are 'natural' in the same way that emotional cries are 'natural' movements of the vocal organs. With practice and experience the ape learns to use his fingers in new ways. This capacity for improvement depends largely on the brain. If the ape does not adapt his vocal capabilities in the same way it is because he has found no particular advantage in doing so. Man, thanks to his still greater capacity, has adapted his digital movements to a thousand new and delicate operations. The process is slow, since each operation has to be acquired in turn, perhaps at long intervals, and the differentiation of muscle, nerve and central organ must proceed harmoniously with, and in reciprocal influence with, the developing behaviour. And so it is with the use of the voice.[3]

Now arbitrary signs can only be understood in a restricted social group. It is only those individuals who are in constant intercourse with one another who will be able to recognize the meaning of the common signs. The most striking thing, therefore, that would distinguish the arbitrary from the 'natural' or self-explanatory signs, would be their unintelligibility to children and strangers. But this property was not without its advantages, for though it might be inconvenient to be unable to converse freely with a stranger, it was also sometimes useful to be able to say something to a companion without being understood by anybody else. Experiences of this kind could bring to notice the important distinction between signs *ex congruo* and signs *ad placitum*. And appreciation of this distinction could lead to attempts to develop both types — a *lingua franca* composed of universally intelligible signs, and a conventional language for private use. The private language, utilizing conventional signs, would be more concise and convenient. The *lingua franca* composed of self-explanatory signs and utilizing gestures, drawings, pantomime and concrete objects or models, would be long-winded and awkward but intelligible without previous agreement.

When imitative signs were used, sounds were among the things which could be most accurately imitated. And when the use of such sounds in intercourse was established there is no reason why abridgment and conventionalization should not take place. But arbitrary sounds produced by the human vocal organs will naturally assume a character specially adapted to those organs. The natural sounds produced by the human voice are not the same as those produced by other animals, by rushing waters, howling winds or pattering rain. These sounds may perhaps be tolerably imitated by the human voice, and primitive races are said to show remarkable powers of mimicry. But even if the accomplishment were more general it would not go far, and as soon as resemblance ceased to be an important property of signs, the natural human vocal sounds would supplant all others.

These natural sounds are the vowel sounds primarily and,

3. Lieberman has recently given evidence that the human speech-producing mechanism is species-specific, and has evolved from something less efficient for noise-making (but more efficient for breathing, chewing and other 'vegetative' functions) in other primates. He allows (following Hewes) that the use of gesture may well have preceded the use of sounds of any kind in human communication, and that the articulate sounds of today were preceded by less efficient sounds produced with a relatively inferior apparatus (Eds.).

under the stress of emotion, almost exclusively. But in play the movements of the tongue and lips would break up the vowel sequence with consonants. The milder and pleasurable emotions could as easily seek expression in movements of the mouth as in dance movements of hands and arms and legs. As Jespersen says:

> It is perfectly possible that speech first developed from something which had no other purpose than that of exercising the muscles of the mouth and throat and amusing oneself and others by the production of pleasant or possibly only strange sounds. The motives for uttering sounds may have changed entirely in the course of centuries without the speakers being at any point conscious of this change within them. (1947, p.437)

This last supposition is perhaps inspired by the anti-rationalist bias which often prompts the modern anthropologist to shrink from any explanation which implies an intelligent motive. But there is no reason why men like other animals should not learn to adapt their impulsive acts for the accomplishment of intelligent purposes. What we cannot explain is how they could manage to adapt a form of behaviour which did not exist. We must therefore assume that the sounds of speech were, at least in part, available before the time came for them to be appropriated to the needs of communication. Once this appropriation had begun, however, there would be a new motive for developing and differentiating to the greatest possible extent the natural products of the voice. Play would do much and provide perhaps the first hint of what was possible, as it has done in so many other cases, but it seems probable that very many refinements and distinctions would result from the needs of language in use.

Now it is one thing to explain how certain arbitrary sounds came to be used as signs and so contribute to the general apparatus of communication, but it is another to explain how such signs could be built up into a complete system which entirely displaced all others. The great difficulty about any conventional system lies in ensuring that all shall use the signs with the same meaning. At the outset such agreement in use could only be obtained among the members of a small and compact community. Moreover, so long as the materials for oral communication were not enough to displace all other signs, the advantages of an exclusively oral language would not be obvious. And the number of words that would be required for all purposes would be so large that the unpractised memory would not be able to retain them. It seems therefore a plausbile theory that oral languages were first cultivated by small groups of men within the community for their special purposes. They could restrict their vocabulary to the special objects of their interest and have the advantage of a secret mode of communication. Under such conditions a few intelligent individuals could experiment and build up more or less extensive vocabularies for their private use. By initiating fresh members into their group they could gradually enlarge the usefulness of the new language.

There is plenty of evidence of the use of secret languages among primitive peoples. Where they are found, different explanations are offered for their use, but the idea of concealment is always involved. Frazer (1911) gives as an example the secret language used during harvest-time by the natives of the Celebes and elsewhere in order not to 'frighten the soul of the rice by revealing to it the alarming truth that it is about to be cut, carried home, boiled and eaten' (p.412). He also mentions Buginese and Macassar sailors who, when passing haunted places, designated common things and actions by 'peculiar terms which are neither Buginese nor Macassar, and therefore cannot be understood by evil spirits, whose knowledge of languages is limited to these two tongues.' (p.413). There is, of course, another reason for avoiding the use of the common names of things. Names, as we shall see in a later chapter, have been widely believed to exert a magical power over their owners, the power to summon them from wherever they may be hiding. To speak of the Devil is to cause him to appear. The inadvertent mention of the name of 'wolf', 'bear', 'snake' may have the effect of bringing these creatures to the spot. The substitution of alternative names implies the belief that one's meaning may be thus disguised. Whether the name produces its effect magically or by being understood in the normal way, this effect can be avoided by avoiding the use of the name.

These cases show that one advantage of oral language has

been often exploited, namely that by means of an easy substitution of terms one can form a system of communication
which is intelligible only to those for whom it is intended. At a
later time writing was found to offer the same advantages, and
codes and cryptograms are today in much more common use
than secret languages. But even now jargons survive in certain
communities, as among tramps and crooks, where their use
may be intended for concealment.

Special languages have been used in secret societies. Johnston mentions initiation societies in the Congo in which
common articles are described by fancy names. There is
nothing in his account to show that the initiates, when they returned to normal life, kept up their special languages. But we
may perhaps presume that their chief purpose was to enable
these people to converse on secret matters without being understood by the uninitiated. Roth tells how Malays addressed
some strange Dyaks in Malay, but spoke to each other (in the
presence of these strangers they did not trust) in what they
called their war language, 'a kind of slang or patter they had
invented, calling things by wrong names' (II, 272).

I have seen no case recorded of any similar artificial gesture-
language. In spite of the arbitrary nature of many of the signs
used in gesture-language it appears, from what is recorded by
Tylor and Wundt, that there is a much more universal character in all the forms of gestural communication, and
wherever it is widely used it is a *lingua franca*. It does not lend
itself to disguise so readily as oral language and conventional
writing. And it seems a plausible suggestion that, at a time
when communication depended still in the main on the language of movement and visible signs, the special advantages of
using conventional *sounds* as the names of certain things
would be exploited. It is certain that such a language could be
developed at first only in a very limited circle. Those who
spoke it must be in constant intercourse with one another; new
words must be quickly made known to the whole community,
duplicates eliminated by a tacit convention, and this would
only be possible in a community so small that each member
would be effectively subject to the influence of the majority.
Perhaps the primitive communities in which language first
developed were small enough to make this possible. If not, we

must suppose that languages were made by restricted groups within a larger community.

It may seem strange to suggest that so useful an invention as oral language should have originated as a means of concealment rather than communication. The advantages of these vocal signs over manual and facial gestures are so great that it might seem absurd to attribute their first introduction to so special a motive as the desire for secrecy. But it must be remembered that the efficiency of speech depends on the existence not only of an extensive vocabulary but also of a linguistic structure. It requires a considerable work of the memory, and the larger the vocabulary the more difficult will it be to extend its use over a large community. Words will only be retained in the memory if frequently used. If all the members of the community are to use the same words with the same meanings they must have frequent opportunity of talking to one another. Thus it seems likely to be long before a vocabulary is accumulated sufficient to make the true advantages of a spoken language felt. A small number of sound-symbols can be used in conjunction with the normal language of movement. This number can be increased for special purposes and by special groups without leading to the adoption of an exclusively oral form of communication.

The task of memory would be lightened to some extent by the effects of sound-symbolism, and sounds may be associated with ideas in more than one way. Much has been written about the relation between the sounds of words and their meanings, and the principle of onomatopoeia has been relied on to account for the origin of language. The view that words originated as imitations of natural sounds, whether human or otherwise, is untenable, if only because of the very limited number of things which possess any sound to imitate. But even words which bear an evident resemblance in sound to the sound which they denote, can often be shown to have a long history and to have existed at an earlier stage in a form so different that all sound similarity vanishes. They cannot therefore have been *invented* with an eye to such suggestive similarity. But whatever its origin, any particular word is easily altered, and chance similarities which result from changes due to other causes may determine a more stable form. Wundt illustrates this by reference to the German words *Rabe* and *Rappe*. The former means 'raven' and is pronounced with a long *a*, the latter 'horse' and has a short *a*. The former may be pronounced in such a way as to suggest the cry of the bird, and the latter to suggest the clatter of horse's hoofs. Now it appears that both words come from an original which was only a bird's name and was pronounced *Rabe* in the North but *Rappe* in the South. Later the word, being specially associated with a *black* bird, came to be used also of a *black* horse. Differentiation then occurred and, if Wundt is right, sound-symbolism determined the use of the two forms of the word. They were not first framed in imitation of their objects, they merely survived, or were more generally adopted, because this association made them easier to remember.

The same thing may be said of all the other kinds of association between word and meaning. It is perhaps seldom that a word is actually invented because of such association. But among the endless different words that come into use from one source or another those tend to survive which for any reason are easier to remember. It is, of course, not *only* the need to avoid burdening the memory that determines the choice of words that remain in use, but this is certainly one important factor; and it accounts for whatever of onomatopoeia or sound-symbolism is to be found in existing languages.

It was pointed out by Wundt that sound-symbolism includes more than onomatopoeia. Certain correspondences between sound and meaning are felt even where no natural sound associated with the meaning exists to explain it. Jespersen (1947) notes that there is a natural association between high tones and brightness, and between low tones and darkness, as for example in 'gleam' and 'gloom'; between the close and thin vowel *i* and small, weak or dainty things; between the length of vowels and emotional attitudes, and so on.

It would be absurd, and Jespersen does not suggest it, to suppose that the words which exemplified such symbolism had been devised for the purpose. All that we can say is that words which have such an advantage over their competitors are more likely to survive. That there are not more such words in our language is due to the fact that there are more important conditions which determine the viability of a word. Words are continually undergoing change in sound and meaning; consequently new symbolic relations arise again and again, and if they aid the memory they will make for the survival of the word. When we have to find expression for our ideas we can only use the words which come to mind. Every association helps to fix a word in our memory, and sound-symbolism is only one of many.

Another important aid to memory results from the assimilation in sound of words which have related meanings. All the regularities of grammar, word-structure, composition and syntax are to be partly explained by this need for economy of memory. The forms, the declensions, the conjugations and rules, do not come into existence as a result of conscious design, but they survive because they are useful.

There is another important case of recourse to mnemonic devices in the use of oral language. Once speech had been firmly established as the normal means of communication it could find its place in communal functions (as well as in converse between individuals) and could thus enter into magical or religious ritual. A brief formula could be used as an invocation or spell, and longer compositions in narrative form could be substituted for dramatic performances. Just as religious performances in dramatic form were based on a more primitive type of communication, so magical liturgies were based on the use of oral language.

In the absence of any kind of phonetic writing these liturgies and narrative spells (on which see p. 122 below) would have to be committed to memory. We have seen how the form of words was influenced by the need to associate them more easily with their meanings. A similar need arose where a sequence of words, perhaps of considerable length, had to be memorized. Here the association had to be, not between each word and its meaning, but between one word and the next; for it was vital, if the utterance was to have its magical virtue, that the right words should be used in the right order.

Now it seems at least plausible to suggest that some of the characteristic features of what has been regarded as poetry through the centuries until the last few decades owe their origin to their mnemonic value. Some kind of rhythm is probably the most common and we may suppose that it was related in the beginning to rhythmical movements of the body, whether these constituted what we should regard as a dance or not. Rhyme, or at least assonance, and alliteration are also common. Repetition of certain groups of words at regular intervals is a feature of a good deal of primitive poetry. Song is usually characterized by the recurrence of the same melody. All these features help the memory.

Compositions of this kind are handed on from one generation to the next without alteration. Not only would they lose their mnemonic features if the words or word-order were changed, but those of them that were enshrined in a religious ritual would lose their magical virtue as well. And we may suppose that they would endure through many generations unchanged. One consequence of this is that the language in which such 'poems' were composed would come in time to differ from the contemporary colloquial speech, for the latter tends to change fairly rapidly where there is no common use of writing. In later times, when all the surviving old poems, which would generally be religious, were to some extent archaic in language and style, this would be thought to be the proper language for poetical composition and attempts would be made to imitate it. The imitation could only be imperfect because it was based on only a very partial acquaintance with the older language. But there resulted a kind of pseudo-archaic 'poetic diction', which was sufficiently arbitrary in character to give rise to the view that a poet might exercise a certain licence in regard to the use of words and the rules of grammar. At the same time the mythical content of the older compositions favoured the idea that poetry was only properly concerned with that kind of material and led poets to give their time and skill to the recital of old legends which had long since ceased to be historically credible or of any religious significance.

In saying that the external features of poetry are largely traceable to features of very early compositions whose function was mnemonic, I do not mean to imply that the features in question were deliberately devised for the purpose of making such compositions easier to remember. But just as the associative links between the sound of words and their meaning were not at first consciously contrived, but simply had a better chance of survival whenever they happened to occur, so we may suppose that the devices of prosody arose at first in a similar manner.

Since early poetical compositions were most often religious, and so associated with religious emotions, it is to some extent understandable that the 'external features' should become associated with the same religious emotions. And this may partially account for the emotional effects of poetry in recent times. Whether it suffices to account for all that has been claimed for poetry is another matter. According to Wordsworth, poetry is '... the first and last of all knowledge—it is as immortal as the heart of man'. Coleridge is even more emphatic. He says that poetry '... is the language of heaven, and in the exquisite delight we derive from poetry we have, as it were, a type, a foretaste, and a prophecy of the joys of heaven'. Such effects seem to require a supernatural explanation, and that I am not prepared to attempt.

Just as we seem able to trace some of the formal characters of poetry to conditions prevailing before writing existed, so, with even more plausibility, we may trace the arts of sculpture and painting back to a time when oral language had not yet been invented. In both cases we trace the characteristic features of the art to devices of a practical nature. In both cases it was magic and religion which first exploited them and challenged the artist to develop his skill, until in time the joy in creation replaced the economic demand.

That, of course, is not the end of the story. But there we must leave it for the present.[4]

I will conclude with a short summary. An oral language must consist for the most part of arbitrary sounds. A few of these may have resulted from the abridgment of natural or imitative sounds, but such a process could not have produced the enormous number of words found in every known language. At some point deliberate invention must have occurred; yet this is conceivable only when man had already come to see how arbitrary sounds *can* be made effective for communica-

---

4.   It can be followed further in the author's article in *Trivium* (1975). See the Bibliography (Eds.).

tion. This they might have learnt from their experience with arbitrary gestures. But since the building up of a language by the invention of words must be a slow process, the real advantages of such a language would not readily appear, and the motive for persevering in such an enterprise would seem to be lacking. We have therefore to look for some other motive which could encourage the use of vocal signs instead of gestures at a time when a language composed exclusively of sounds was still out of the question. This motive, I suggest, might be found in the use of conventional sounds for the sake of secrecy. In restricted groups of men a small number of such sounds could be used, not as a complete language for all purposes, but as a private supplement to the normal language of gesture. There is no reason why such vocal signs should not form part of the normal mode of communication among all the members of the community. But the more such speech forms were multiplied, the more restricted would be their use, and it seems likely that only in small and intimate circles with special private interests would the necessary incentive be found for the deliberate construction of a real language of sounds. But once such a language had come into existence it might be learnt by an ever increasing number of young people, and in course of time it could be degraded into the common language, a new one being invented, if required, for secret communication.

We have seen, finally, that various mnemonic devices have been adopted to link the sound of a word with its meaning, though the proportion of words having such a property must always have been very small. Similarly, where whole sentences or longer verbal sequences had to be memorized, as in religious rituals, methods came into use for linking *successive* words in the memory. This led to the use of certain patterns of composition which survived in poetry after the invention of writing had otherwise made them superfluous.

CHAPTER 10

The Structure of Oral Language

(i) Words, Ideas and Things

It is sometimes stated that there is a symbolic correspondence between the forms of language and the 'structure' of the events or conditions it is used to describe. Wittgenstein says (4.014):

> The gramophone record, the musical thought, the score, the waves of sound, all stand to one another in that pictorial internal relation, which holds between language and the world. To all of them the logical structure is common.

This can only mean that there is the same kind of correspondence between language and everything which it describes as there is between the groove on the disc and the sounds it records. By classing language with mathematics as a form of symbolism, Ogden and Richards apparently favour the same opinion. And Suzanne Langer says that 'syntax is simply the logical form of our language, which copies as closely as possible the logical form of our thought'. She adds: 'To understand language is to appreciate the analogy between the syntactical construct and the complex of ideas, letting the former function as a representative, or "logical picture", of the latter' (p.31). The conception is made a little more concrete by Bertrand Russell in a passage which she quotes:

> In every proposition and every inference there is, besides the particular subject-matter concerned, a certain form, a way in which the constituents of the proposition or inference are put together. If I say, 'Socrates is mortal', 'Jones is angry'. 'The sun is hot' there is something in common in these three cases, something indicated by the word 'is'.

What is common is the form of the proposition, not an actual constituent.

He goes on to suggest that the form may be retained even when all the words are altered, provided that the alteration is performed in stages. His example is:

Socrates drank the hemlock.
Coleridge drank the hemlock.
Coleridge drank opium.
Coleridge ate opium.

Whether there is any significance in the fact that Socrates and Coleridge were both men, that drinking and eating are similar biological processes, and hemlock and opium are both poisonous plant extracts, does not appear. But if the form of the sentence is determined simply by the syntactical structure without reference to the meaning of the words, then we must hold that the following sentences have all the same form:

John has a cold.
Mary has a hat.
Tom has an idea.
Bill has a lesson.
Henry has a drink.
Jane has an objection.

Yet, since they have no common element of meaning, the common word having a different sense in each case, it is difficult to see to what 'logical form of thought' this 'syntactical construct' can correspond.

This notion that the grammatical or syntactical form of a sentence corresponds in some systematic way to the character of the idea which it expresses underlies a great deal of what is called 'logic'. It is based on the illusion that language is, or can be, a symbolic 'system'. That this is in fact an illusion, has, I hope, been made clear above (p. 45). The idea that the structure of language is to be compared with the structure of mathematics is due to a fundamental misconception of the nature of language; also, perhaps, to the vague notion which some people have of the nature of mathematical 'form'. This calls for a few words of explanation.

In the three expressions:

$$\frac{(a+b)^2}{ab} \; ; \qquad \frac{(x+y)^2}{xy} \; ; \qquad \frac{(\cos A + \sin A)^2}{\cos A \sin A} \; ;$$

the a and b, and x and y and the $\cos A$ and $\sin A$, which are called the 'arguments', do not form part of the structure, and may be replaced by any other symbols denoting quantities, however complex. But the brackets, the index, and the position of the arguments in relation to these and one another, together constitute the structure. Now these expressions may be subjected to various transformations according to the rules of algebra. Thus we may put

$$\frac{(a+b)^2}{ab} = \frac{a^2+b^2}{ab} + 2$$

or

$$\frac{(a+b)^2}{ab} = \frac{a+b}{a} + \frac{b+a}{b}$$

and so on. And if such transformations are valid for a and b, then they are valid for any other arguments such as x and y or $\cos A$ and $\sin A$, or any other expressions however complicated. They concern the form of the expression and not the arguments. Particular forms of this kind are called functions. If we write the symbol F for the function, and put

$$F(a,b) = \frac{(a+b)^2}{ab}$$

then we have also:

$$F(\alpha,\beta) = \frac{(\alpha+\beta)^2}{\alpha\beta}$$

and so on.

Now when it is asserted that propositions expressed in ordinary language have a *form* which may be distinguished from the content just as the form of a mathematical expression may be distinguished from the arguments of the function, we have to ask in what the form of a sentence consists and how it may be separated from the 'actual constituents'.

It is reasonable enough to distinguish the words of a sentence from the order in which they are arranged; but grammarians go further than this, and recognize three elements in linguistic structure: vocabulary, accidence and syntax. In addition they classify words into a number of 'parts of speech', noun, verb, etc. The rules of accidence state how words are modified or 'inflected' in different circumstances. The rules of syntax determine the arrangement of words in a sentence. The definition of the parts of speech informs us of the various functions of different kinds of word. But these rules are not the same in different languages and it is impossible to generalize them. Yet, if we are to find anything in all this analogous to mathematical form, generalization is essential.

Let us review briefly the three elements of word-formation, inflexion and sentence construction, more especially with reference to English, to see what part of the total meaning is contributed by each, how far the contributions are independent, and to what extent, if at all, we may speak of a linguistic form in the same sense in which we speak of mathematical form.

Communication is concerned with things—material things, persons, feelings, desires, fears, and so on, and with the relations between them. These relations are not indefinitely numerous and are to a large extent determined by the nature of the things. If a communication includes the words for *tree* and *axe*, or for *wood* and *fire*, or for *river* and *fish*, the listener can at once supply from his own knowledge the most important relations which link the two ideas. We cannot suppose that at an early stage oral language could represent adequately and unambiguously for any listener every possible sequence of ideas. The interpretation of every communication would depend largely on the implications of the common situation and the known relations between the things named. The words alone would suffice without the aid of any syntactical devices. Even now the rules of grammar and syntax may often be ignored without the communication becoming unintelligible. If, for example, the witness of a road accident, being a foreigner and imperfectly acquainted with our language, should report as follows, 'Dog, cat, chase, bus, lamppost, avoid, crash', his hearers would have little difficulty in understanding his meaning. The mention of lampposts and buses at once limits the possibilities to a street, and the ideas evoked by all the other words are already related to one another in their minds. It is known that dogs chase cats and not vice versa. And it is more likely that a bus should crash into a lamppost in trying to avoid a dog than that a lamppost should crash into a dog in trying to chase a bus. Such inferences are based on common knowledge which may always be assumed under the normal conditions of communication.

Nevertheless it is clear that as the scope of language was extended, as the number of topics and ideas as well as the number and variety of people involved increases, it must become less and less possible to rely on common knowledge to make sense of a string of words without special arrangement or connecting links. But before considering the possibilities available to supplement the meaning of the words I will illustrate by a short passage the general nature of the contribution of these structural elements to the meaning.

The passage is taken from Lane's *Arabian Nights*. The order of the words is changed completely; all particles are omitted: every word is put in its least inflected form; and there is no punctuation: 'Aladdin Baghdad dog street evening dark door mosque vestibule arise proceed enter pass walk see conceal bark.' Such a string of words, though it may vaguely suggest a number of possible scenes, certainly does not convey any definite meaning. If we knew the whole story up to and after this particular scrambled sentence, it might be fairly easy to supply the missing structure. But let us now see what difference is produced by restoring the proper order, while still omitting inflexions, particles and punctuation: 'Aladdin arise proceed enter Baghdad dog bark Aladdin pass street evening walk dark see door mosque enter vestibule mosque conceal Aladdin vestibule.' In this version I have replaced pronouns by the nouns they stand for, and already the meaning begins to be dimly recognizable. We now go a step further and insert the essential punctuation. This serves to show which words belong together and is, perhaps, the most important single element in linguistic structure. In the spoken language it is replaced by pauses and varying intonation.

> Aladdin arise, proceed, enter Baghdad. Dog bark Aladdin Aladdin pass street, evening, Aladdin walk dark, Aladdin see door mosque, enter vestibule mosque, conceal Aladdin vestibule.

By breaking up the whole into brief portions we greatly reduce the number of possible meanings. The meaning of each short sequence is suggested by the words themselves and the obvious relations between the ideas they denote. As the number of words, and therefore ideas, increases, the number of possible relations rapidly increases. By dividing a passage of twenty words into four short groups, we obtain four ideas to combine instead of twenty, and if each group carries an obvious meaning the task of interpretation will be reduced to divining the connexion between these four ideas.

The words which have been retained in the above transcription I call substantive words. They convey a tolerably definite idea even in isolation. The words omitted are structural elements or 'particles', and they, together with the inflexions, the punctuation and the word-order constitute the structure or form of language. Let us now compare these simplified word sequences with the complete passage:

> Then arising, he proceeded, and entered Baghdad. The dogs barked behind him as he passed through the streets, and in the evening, while he was walking on in the dark, he saw the door of a mosque, and entering its vestibule, he concealed himself in it.

Now in this example at least it will be seen that the meaning of the passage depends only to a small extent on the particles and inflexions. This does not mean, however, that these elements, which appear to be found in all languages, could be easily dispensed with, especially in more complex descriptions or explanations. The distinction between word and phrase and between particle and inflexion is by no means always clear, and in unwritten languages disappears. In written languages words are fixed by the common usage of writers, printers and lexicographers. In the written language 'loving' and 'given' are inflected words, whereas 'to give' and 'in love' are phrases containing particles, but in the spoken language it would be impossible to make such a distinction.

(ii) Composition of Words

I have said that the structure of language consists of the particles and the word-order, but we might see another element of structure in word-composition. Moreover many substantive words have a common element of form which corresponds to a common element of meaning. It was pointed out in an earlier chapter that one of the fundamental principles in communication by signs is that of combination. Something that cannot be expressed by any single sign may be at once suggested by a combination. The signs may be combined so as to suggest the combination of two ideas or the abstraction of a common feature. In any particular case, given the meaning of the components, the resultant will in general be evident, as with such words as 'coalshed', 'seaweed', 'penwiper' or 'toothpick'. The relation between coal and shed is quite different from that between sea and weed or tooth and pick. If simple juxtaposition of two words makes a new word which is unambiguous it is because of the known relations between things, not because of anything in the word, the manner of composition, or the nature of the sounds. The *order* of the components may, of course, indicate their relation, as in English, where the first component usually has an adjectival force. Thus a coalshed is a kind of shed, not a kind of coal.

Now the general principle, which is fundamental for all communication, may be stated as follows. In order to convey a complex piece of information for which there exists no agreed symbol the agent must select certain elements from the whole for which he does possess signs, and by combining these he must rely on the respondent to infer from them the whole. If the respondent can in fact do this it is because his experience and stock of ideas are similar to those of the agent, so that the same mental habits which lead the one to analyse a complex idea into certain elements lead the other to recombine those elements into the same complex idea.

A particular real occurrence may be analysed in many different ways. Each observer sees in it a somewhat different combination of elements, for the elements into which he analyses it must be represented in his own experience and in his memory. Moreover if he wishes to describe the occurrence to another he is restricted not only to components he can recognize, but to those of them for which he happens to have signs. And whether his description suffices in fact to convey the information intended will depend also on whether his respondent is familiar with the signs, attaches to them similar ideas, and can from his experience reconstruct out of those component ideas the same original whole. Thus the possibility of communication is not dependent on a minute analysis of phenomena nor on the existence of a multitude of signs, but on the community of ideas and habits between the communicating parties. An English chemist with but a limited knowledge of German may manage fairly well to exchange ideas with a German chemist. But mere acquaintance with the German language, however extensive, will not enable an Englishman to follow the expositions of the German chemist if it is not supported by any knowledge of the elements of chemistry.

The examples I have considered so far have been composite words the components of which could be used separately. But there are many which contain components which cannot be so used. These components may have a constant meaning or contribute something recognizable to the various words in which they occur. Thus the first syllable in such words as 'unhappy' has a constant negative force, and the suffix '-able' may be said to convert the verbs 'believe', 'desire' into 'what may be believed', 'what may be desired', etc. In the same way the words 'thoughtful', 'hopeful' may be said to have a common element of meaning which is due to the final syllable. This kind of thing is common to a great many languages, perhaps to all.

Now here is something which looks like systematic symbolism. The suffixes '-able' and '-ful' might perhaps be regarded as a kind of *operators* which, though without meaning in isolation, are nevertheless able to affect in a definite way all words to which they are attached. But unfortunately for this view such systematic symbolism is never carried out consistently. It is partly a matter of convention. Thus we say 'adjustable' but not 'regulatable', 'irritable' but not 'annoyable', 'assailable' but not 'assaultable'. But it is partly a question of meaning, as intransitive verbs would give meaningless words with this suffix, and many transitive verbs, like 'ask', 'add', 'act', 'affect', seem not to require such a derivative.

Other suffixes have a less constant meaning. 'Imaginative' and 'talkative' are used of persons given to imagining things or to talking, 'restorative' and 'laxative' of medicines whose function is to restore or to relax. 'Comparative', 'qualitative', 'relative' and 'negative' are used in a more general way signifying some connexion with comparison, quality, relation and negation. In other cases this suffix is replaced by others — e.g. 'fanciful', 'quarrelsome', 'flattering', 'consolatory', and so on. In many cases, instead of a derivative from an English verb, some adjective of French or Latin origin is used, as in the case of 'credulous', 'pugnacious', 'audacious', which stand for the verbs 'believe', 'fight' and 'dare'.

Prefixes in English have as a rule a rather more definite meaning than suffixes, although the same prefix may have more than one meaning (e.g. overweight, overboard, overhear, oversee). Now even if a particular prefix has twenty distinct meanings in its various compounds, this does not prevent it from serving a useful purpose. If each of the different meanings is represented in a dozen words the burden on the memory will be to that extent reduced. Even if only two words have at the same time a common element of meaning and a common element of form, this will constitute an economy for the memory. The advantage is not destroyed by the lack of consistency. In view of the endless variety of ideas for which our words stand it could not be expected that exactly the same modification should be applicable to any large number of them. If by the addition of prefixes we could change the meaning of 'walk' into 'run', 'canter', 'trot' and 'gallop', to how many other words could the same prefixes be added so as to produce a like change of meaning? In some other languages more is done in this way than in English. But where the parallel modifications do not exist in the real world there is no advantage in having parallel modifications in the form of our words.

Turning now to the particles, we shall consider first the meaning of our common prepositions. Taking account only of the outward form of the words we can construct any number of phrases having exactly the same structure. Thus:

The author of this book.
The lid of this box.
The winner of this event.

It might be supposed, from what has been said by Bertrand Russell, that the common form bears some common meaning. Yet all that can be said is that *some* kind of relation is implied between the two 'arguments'. What the relation is is certainly not indicated by the preposition, since it is quite different in each case, and is indicated solely by the meaning of the substantive words. It is only because we know the meaning of 'author' and 'book' that we can see the meaning of 'of'. If we replace the preposition in these phrases by 'in', 'to', 'at', 'by' or 'on', the result is not any uniform change in the meaning, but in most cases merely a solecism. Where the change produces a permissible English phrase the meaning sometimes remains the same.

Some prepositions have a more restricted use than these six, and may have a more constant meaning, as do those denoting position, like 'under', 'over', 'inside', 'outside', 'between', 'among'. Here we may say that the meaning remains the same whatever noun follows. However, some of these prepositions have what grammarians call metaphorical or figurative uses, and in consequence do not admit of transformation by substitution of another preposition denoting position. Every student of a foreign language knows that such 'idioms' cannot be expected to follow the English model. The reader may feel that there is some relation between these different uses and that they do have some connexion with the 'concrete' meaning of the word. But it would be difficult indeed to give an account of this common meaning; and the feeling that there exists an analogy may well derive from the custom of using the same word. It is only when we learn that in other languages a different set of analogies must be assumed that we realize the purely conventional nature of the relation.

Some languages make a much clearer distinction between prepositions and conjunctions than English, where they are often interchangeable. Indeed, but for the fact that Englishmen in the past, at least English grammarians, have studied Latin or French, they would hardly have discovered the difference. We say 'after breakfast' and also 'after I have had breakfast'. In the first we use, according to the grammarians, a preposition, in the second a conjunction, although both the meaning and the form of the word is the same. Conjunctions sometimes help to suggest the relation between the substantive words, but they can do this very inadequately unless the substantive words by their own meaning suggest the relation. The conjunctions 'that', 'as', 'but' convey in many contexts no more meaning than the prepositions 'by' or 'in' or 'to'. It is this absence of any precise meaning which makes these little words so important in metaphysics and theology.

Their lack of precise meaning, however, does not make these particles by any means useless in intelligible discourse, for in oral language it is necessary in some way to indicate, in a long sequence of substantive words, which are to be taken as connected in meaning. And prepositions and conjunctions, being few and short and of very indefinite meaning, serve very well as links to join the substantive words into intelligible groups. The possible relations between the things denoted by substantive words are so diverse and numerous that it would not be possible to have a special particle for every relation. Hence the particles have with a few exceptions lost whatever specific meaning they may have once possessed and play much the same rôle in a word-sequence that the syllable plays in a word. As we have seen, some syllables do have a certain independent significance, but in general it may be said that they are meaningless except in combination.

Enough has perhaps been said to show that there is no systematic correspondence between the forms of language and its meanings. What correspondence exists is partial, local and inconsistent. The same principle applies here as in the case of sound-symbolism. Analogy may arise in different ways by chance, and when it is recognized it is welcomed for its mnemonic value, or it impresses itself on the memory in successful rivalry with alternative forms. The fact that such analogies have no general application does not make them valueless. Other associations, other analogies arise in relation to other parts of the language and are exploited in the same way without there being any attempt to reconcile them or bring them under a general rule. Such a systematizing effort would only be conceivable to a few exceptional minds, and once the use of oral language had spread beyond the limits of a restricted group the influence of the few would cease to count.

Thus, in order to explain the development of these elements of linguistic structure, we have not to look for any far-reaching design and need not resort to any theory of divine inspiration. The same principle applies here as in the case of other inventions. The lucky act and the lucky situation must be given; the genius of the inventor lies in his power of seeing that they may be exploited. In the case of language there must have been innumerable inventors, since everyone in trying to express himself is forced at times to invent, and novelties of expression thus introduced would be copied. Out of the resulting competition there would grow up a common language among all those who remained in regular intercourse with one another, full of anomalies but mitigated by limited rules and analogical forms which lightened the task of memory.

I have said nothing yet about grammatical inflexions. In English they play only a minor part and could without much inconvenience be dispensed with. In some languages they seem to have disappeared entirely. On the other hand Russian, and to a less extent the other Slavonic languages, have still a considerable inflexional apparatus comparable to what is found in Sanskrit, Greek and Latin. It was at one time believed that inflexional languages were in some way superior to languages like English or Danish in which the function of the inflexions seems to have been taken over by the particles. The ground for this belief was probably the traditional respect for the classical languages, reinforced by the discovery that the chief European languages could be regarded as belonging to the same family as Sanskrit and Greek.

It is easy to see that an inflexion can serve the same purpose as a particle, and in a language which has never been reduced to writing it is impossible to make the distinction. In spoken English, prepositions are often attached to their noun or pronoun as securely as any inflexion. In the French phrase 'Je lui dirai . . .' there is nothing in the pronunciation which distinguishes the particle 'lui' from the inflexion '-ai' except that one precedes and the other follows the substantive word 'dire'.

In translating from a highly inflexional language like Greek into English we often have to use a preposition instead of an inflexion. The genitive 'soma*tos*' must be translated by some such phrase as 'of the body', 'than the body' etc. If the English word 'of' were always to be translated by the inflexion '-os' then the only difference would be that the significant syllable preceded the noun in the one case and followed in the other. But for one thing the Greek inflexion cannot always be translated by the same English preposition. And whatever English preposition is correctly here represented by '-os', is not always represented by the same inflexion in other Greek nouns, which form their genitives in a great variety of different ways. Thus, if the inflexion served no other purpose than to replace the particle, it would seem to have great disadvantages. It is easier to learn one word and apply it generally than to memorize a number of alternative inflexions. The same can be said of the verbal inflexions. In English we express the future by the particles 'shall' or 'will' — incidentally a meaningless distinction — while in Latin and Greek we have to learn a great many different inflexions. Yet this great variety of forms has no bearing on the meaning.

There is, however, another purpose served by these inflexions. The principle of *concord* allows a connexion between words to be indicated even when they are separated in the sentence by several other words. The particle must be placed alongside the word to which it belongs and can only fulfil its function if the words it links are suitably arranged. But the principle of concord may make such arrangement unnecessary. The 'agreement', for example, between adjective and noun serves to show which adjective is to be taken with which noun, without its being necessary for the two words to stand side by side. Nevertheless, nothing could be much less systematic than the Latin and Greek declensions, and had understanding really depended on the working of such a system the language could never have been used for anything but poetry and philosophy. But once again it has to be said that because this method of concord was inadequate it does not follow that as an auxiliary it was not useful. Even in its much reduced form in modern French and Italian it is still possible to gain a little conciseness by exploiting the distinction of gender and agreement of pronouns, where in English the ambiguous 'it' has to be replaced by a circumlocution.

In Swahili there is a somewhat similar system in which the nouns are distributed into nine classes, each class having a characteristic prefix or initial letter, one for the singular and another for the plural. Adjectives receive the corresponding initial to show their agreement. There is apparently nothing that corresponds to the Latin cases, but the increased number of classes may to some extent compensate for this defect. The personal prefixes of the verbs are also determined by the class of nouns to which the subject, or sometimes the object, belongs. The demonstrative pronouns 'this' and 'that' are given the same suffixes when they refer to nouns of this class. The system sounds elaborate but, as might be expected, it seems in practice to be full of inconsistencies and ambiguities.

No doubt other languages contain other devices of the same kind, the common purpose of which is to link together all those words in a sentence which, for interpretation, must be taken as a connected group. The personal endings of the verb serve in the same way, however inadequately, to link it to its subject. In colloquial communication this is useful, in forensic it rarely serves any purpose, for it depends upon a classification of the universe into three classes (the speaker, the person addressed and the remainder of the universe). The distinction between singular and plural is more useful, but it is clearly not necessary, for it is often not made. None of these devices seems to be indispensable, and even the particles can be omitted if the substantive words are carefully chosen and arranged in short sequences. The language of telegrams need not be more ambiguous than a flowing literary style. If skill is used in composition, if pauses are placed between portions of the sentence which are to be considered as wholes, if so far as possible words connected in meaning are placed together, and if the words themselves are chosen not only for their general meaning but also with a view to their context, so that they and their neighbours may illumine one another, then we can do very well without inflexions and even at a pinch without particles.

(iii) Grammar and Thought

There remains the question of the parts of speech and the forms by which in some languages they are distinguished. Let us consider in particular the adjective and the noun. It has generally been supposed that nouns and adjectives are the names of different kinds of thing, and that this is the ground on which formal distinction rests when it is found. Yet it is hard to explain what kind of thing is denoted by an adjective. Jespersen holds that the distinction between noun and adjective 'must have some intrinsic reason, some logical or psychological ('notional') foundation' (1924, chapter 5), since it is a very widespread distinction (even though less clear in some languages than in others) and since, wherever it occurs, the same words are mostly found in the same category. Thus the words which denote the ideas black and white, tall and short, sweet and sour, hot and cold, are always characterized by the adjectival form. Must there not be something in the meanings of these words which determines this uniformity of treatment in different languages? Yet what is it? In many languages adjectives may be freely formed from nouns. Such words as 'foolish', 'childish' signify the properties of a fool or a child. It must, in these cases, be the way in which the words are used and not their meaning, which makes them into adjectives. On the other hand it is often as easy to make a noun out of an adjective. The noun still denotes exactly the same properties as the adjective, but is not used in the same way.

How then *is* the adjective used? The grammarians usually say that it qualifies a noun, that it limits the connotation of the noun. The expression 'tall man' does not include in its meaning as many individuals as the single word 'man', and 'white horse' applies to fewer animals than 'horse'. Can we then say that any word which limits the meaning of a noun is an adjective? Certainly not if we accept the determinations of the dictionary. 'A game-keeper's dog' and a 'blackbird's nest' are similar expressions in which 'dog' and 'nest' are qualified by nouns. Jespersen (1924, p. 75) suggests that the adjective has a wider meaning than the noun, and says that whereas the *extension* of the noun is less than that of the adjective, its intension is greater. Thus the noun 'violet' denotes an object having very many different qualities, whereas the adjective 'violet' denotes only a single quality. There are many more violet objects in the world than the flower of that name. The noun stands for a smaller number of things but implies a great deal more in the things it does stand for. This may seem plausible though it does not amount to a clear distinction since extension and intension are matters of degree. And there are some words, universally recognized as adjectives by grammarians, which are more special than others equally universally held to be nouns. Thus we speak of a 'human hair', a 'lunar eclipse', or 'terrestrial magnetism'. In English many adjectives are in no way formally distinguished from nouns. Thus in 'gold watch' and 'clay pipe', 'gold' and 'clay' are adjectives — from the grammarian's point of view. But in 'pipe clay' it is 'pipe' which is the adjective. Neither intension or extension of the words has changed. In such phrases according to the English convention it is always the first which is the adjective. But this implies that there is a distinction. What is it? It is not the comparative extension or intension of the word taken in isolation, but rather the question whether the word in a given combination is used to limit the meaning of the other. A 'parrot cage' is a certain kind of cage, a 'gold watch' a certain kind of watch; whereas in the phrase 'cage parrot' it is the word 'cage' which restricts the meaning of the noun.

The relation between ideas which underlies the grammatical distinction is real enough, and has in fact given rise to the various grammatical forms which in many languages serve to distinguish the adjective from the noun. But languages become stereotyped while the needs and ideas of those who use them develop. It is only the professional grammarians who are interested in consistency, or even have enough knowledge to appreciate what it means. Words most commonly used in the adjectival sense, that is to say to limit the meaning of other words, come to have distinct forms or endings. But there is no law of man or nature to ensure that no other words shall be used in the same way.

It may be asked why a special form should ever be required since English practice shows that it is easily dispensed with. There must of course be many particular answers to this question which apply to different languages. But there is one general answer which may well apply to a great many. It is important, when two words are brought together in this way, to make quite clear which is playing the part of substantive and which of adjective. In English it is done by word-order, and a special adjective ending would serve the same purpose. In French the order is usually reversed (the adjective following the noun) and the form of the word is more often distinctive.

The practical requirement which all these forms and methods serve, each in its limited way, is description. The number of words at our disposal is very small in comparison with the number of things and events which we need to describe. How can we make the most economical and effective use of the words we have? When we want to describe a thing we do not attempt to analyse it into its simplest parts or qualities, but get as near to it as we can with a single word and then correct or qualify with the help of additional words. The way in which we do this depends on what we are describing. If we want to describe a tiger we do not begin by saying it is striped, for this restricts our hearer's field of thought hardly at all. But if we say it is a big cat we have already indicated a thousand 'qualities' in two words. Sometimes the limiting word may denote a simple quality, while the substantive denotes all the rest. Thus 'a black horse' conveys a fairly clear idea. In such phrases as 'suspension bridge', 'steam ship', 'kitchen sink', 'garden path', the limiting words denote qualities as complex as those denoted by the substantives. Perhaps some logicians would hesitate to regard 'kitchen' as a quality of a sink, or 'garden' as a quality of a path, but the logical distinction between substance and quality which has so much exercised the metaphysicians is as illusory as that between adjective and noun.

Philosophers have sometimes held that the difference

between substance and quality lies in the fact that the latter cannot exist apart from the former. Whereas a *thing* may continue to exist after losing one or more of its qualities, a *quality* cannot exist apart from some thing. White cotton can be dyed red and red cotton bleached. The cotton remains while its properties come and go. But this is a philosophical abstraction. More naive people have always recognized that qualities can be transferred from one object to another. The real ground of the philosophical abstraction is merely linguistic usage. Because we cannot, in many languages, make the adjective the subject of a proposition, or at least of a grammatical sentence — philosophers and logicians are apt to confound these — it is felt that a 'quality' cannot have an independent existence. We cannot say that 'small' or 'blue' or 'happy' exists. But it is really only the adjectival form of the word that prevents us. We can speak of the Welsh mountains, the pulmonary vein, the autumnal equinox, atomic weights, terrestrial magnetism, an electric current, or parental affection. True we cannot say that parental exists, nevertheless there exist parents. And there is nothing unreal about the earth, about Wales, about the lungs, autumn, atoms and electricity. These 'things' become 'qualities' as soon as we find it convenient to use the words for that purpose.

Thus, though we may recognize a certain distinction between substance and quality, somewhat arbitrary but often useful, and though the adjectival form of words is commonly associated with the latter, the conceptual distinction is long subsequent to the grammatical formation, and the two do not coincide. Hence attempts to define the grammatical relation in terms of a conceptual distinction are vain. The needs of description lead to the apposition of words which separately do not suffice but which, taken together, may suggest what is intended. For this purpose words may be combined in several ways, and one important mode of combination consists in first choosing a word which comes as near as possible to denoting the thing to be described and then adding other words which correct the defects of the first. It was from this purely practical method of description that originated the old logical distinction between *genus* and *differentia*. But it was an error if Aristotle or any of his followers supposed that it rested on anything except practical convenience.

It will be found, I think, that the other parts of speech, so far as they are distinguishable by their form or the way in which they are associated with other words, although they too have a definite relation to certain aspects of the real world, are yet not capable of being correlated at all exactly with these. In the first place the number of distinct parts of speech recognizable by their form is quite small, whereas there is an infinite variety of phenomena for the description of which language is used. Nouns and verbs may correspond roughly to things and actions, but the real world cannot be so simply classified. And the grammatical distinction, as in the case of adjectives, is not consistent. Actions are as often expressed by nouns as by verbs, and many verbs express states, conditions or qualities and no action at all. The verbal forms were perhaps first associated with words denoting human actions, and for that reason we find the very widespread distinction between the three persons. The fact that human actions commonly involve some object or instrument has determined another general feature of verbal syntax. For when these forms were later applied to words that denoted natural phenomena of all kinds, a mutual influence was exerted no doubt by anthropomorphic conceptions and grammatical conceptions. Language, first adapted for the description of human behaviour, was later used for more general purposes, and its early form influenced not only the manner of describing but also the manner of conceiving other phenomena.

This discussion must surely have made it obvious, if it was not so before, that the complexity of the real world cannot be systematically represented by any language. The kind of symbolical representation which is possible in mathematics, because there all ideas are combined out of a small number of elements, is in language quite impossible. But this is not due to a deficiency in the number of signs or sounds available, but to the limits of the memory and the time needed for establishing conventions. If we assume that there are fifty distinct vocal sounds available and that we form all our words of ten sounds or less, over ten thousand million words could be formed—far greater than the number that have been used in any language. If we assume that every language contains a hundred thousand words there would be needed one hundred thousand such languages, no two of which had a single common word, in order to make up the total. And we may fairly assume that no individual would require to express so many thoughts. For if a separate word were used for every distinct thought, this supply would suffice for a man who lived to be a hundred if he conceived three ideas per second and never thought the same thought twice. It is clear that it is not the difficulty of constructing words which is the cause of the inadequacy of language.

What we need is the ability to express ourselves with the aid of a comparatively small number of distinct words. In mathematics we have a small number of symbols, a, b, c, &c., which represent quantities, and we can combine these symbols in as many ways as quantities can be combined or related. Hence the symbolism of mathematics may be said to correspond with the complexity of the things symbolized. But although by means of language we are able in general to convey to a listener or reader most of our ideas, so long as they correspond approximately to the elements or features of our common environment, yet there is no settled and consistent correlation between words and ideas, between language and thought.

I will conclude this chapter with a review of the argument. We may suppose the number of distinct words to be unlimited. In connected discourse however they can only be arranged in sequence. If we had a word for every thought or every combination of ideas that we needed to express, then we should never need to use more than one word at a time, and we should never be at a loss, as long as our memory served us. But in real life we have no comprehensive words like this and have to make up sentences, and the main business of language consists in just this putting together of words into new combinations to express new thoughts. That any idea, however complicated, so long as it is derived from experience of the real world, can be *denoted* by a set of words is not to be questioned. The simplest sound is just as adequate as a sentence or a treatise, once the meaning has been established and agreed by all who use the language. The problem of language lies not in the use of such words, once the meaning is settled, but in the settlement of the meanings, and in the expression of ideas to which no words or phrases have as yet been conventionally assigned.

Discourse consists in putting together familiar words so as to suggest in the mind of the listener more or less complex ideas. But the most familiar words have as a rule the most general and uncertain meanings. Not only is one word used in very many different ways, but its diversity of uses is not exactly the same for every member of the community. A combination of words suggests a combination of ideas. But only the inherent probabilities of a particular situation enable us to guess how the ideas are to be combined. It is quite impossible to show by any consistent linguistic device in the arrangement or inflexion of words what relation is intended between the ideas denoted by the separate words. We can merely experiment with different combinations until we see the desired idea take shape in the mind of our companion. And our only means of recognizing this is through the interpretation in turn of what he says to us. It is remarkable indeed, not that misunderstandings occur, but rather that we manage to understand one another at all. And it is probably true that we seldom do understand one another more than partially, except in relation to the most normal and regular circumstances of life. Our abstract and general ideas are rarely communicable, at least by means of words, for we have not in our various minds the common basis to make communication possible. In scientific questions where complex relations between things are involved, we resort to gestures or picture-writing, and demonstrate by visible actions whatever we have to convey. Words only become a possible medium for scientific intercourse after the essential ideas have been conveyed by practical demonstration, physical experiment, diagrams and mathematical explanations. It is through sight and touch, in conjunction with our own manipulations, that we acquire the ideas to which we learn to attach words. Only when we have first acquired the ideas can we understand any verbal communication concerning them.

CHAPTER 11

Language and Magic

A significant development in the history of human inventions has been the vast accumulation of erroneous beliefs and ineffectual practices. The behaviour of apes furnishes many examples of error and the misapplication of acquired skill; but such mistakes grow out of the individual's own experience and his own misjudgment. Among men the potent new factors of imitation and communication, while they make the inventions of the few available to the many, give rise also to the human specialities of myth and magic. For the ape belief can only concern the structure of the present situation and can reach but a short way into the past, the future or the remote, and in consequence error, if not fatal, will generally be corrected. But where belief extends beyond the range of experimental testing there is little guarantee against illusion. The development of the mental powers which resulted in profitable inventions gave rise, as a by-product, to magic and hocus-pocus. In this process language played an important part.

Some writers seem to have supposed that the remarkable beliefs of the kind usually called magical can be accounted for only by assuming a special kind of primitive psychology. Frazer writes sometimes as if primitive man is by nature constrained to draw wrong inferences. Yet we know that this same primitive man invented many important things. He discovered the uses of fire, domesticated the dog, invented language, pottery, weaving and agriculture. In these he showed a normal psychological endowment. According to Childe, the available archaeological evidence suffices to indicate that 'magic practices were combined with technical operations even in prehistoric times'. And if we assume some peculiar mental trait to account for the magic we only make it more difficult to explain the genuine discoveries. The truth is that early man's errors were due to the same characters and circumstances as the errors of modern scientists and philosophers.[1] The vain contrivances of early men were the by-product of their restless explorations, the result of over-eager inductions, and not due to any peculiarity in their logical processes. Most types of magical belief can be traced to a genuine discovery. Some analogies are fruitful and lead to scientific generalizations; others are deceptive and lead to sorcery, fetishism and myth.

If we consider the principal types of magical belief and practice in relation to the contemporary acquaintance with the real world, we see that they may be accounted for as the result of premature induction. Since this is more easily shown in the less primitive forms I shall begin with these; but that this is a principle of wide generality appears when it is shown that the mass of beliefs classed by Frazer as 'contagious' and 'homoeopathic' magic can be brought within the same formula. I shall show that just as astrology, alchemy and medicinal magic arise from an unjustified extension of principles based on the observation of genuine correlations in the realms of astronomy, chemistry and pathology, so other more primitive forms of magic were related to early discoveries in the art of communication. For it will appear that there is a striking analogy between the forms of primitive magic and the primitive forms of communication.

Many plants are found from experience to yield medicines and poisons. Applied externally or taken internally they have unmistakable and constant effects, sometimes agreeable and sometimes not. The real connexion between the herb and its effects is unknown, though some character of form or colour may be suggestive. But it is a logical and normal process of induction to argue that, since so many plants are found to produce interesting effects on the human body, there is no *a priori* reason why we should not be able to discover a plant to

---

1.   The view expressed here is in direct opposition to a widespread belief, typified by the statement in the article 'Magic, primitive' in the *Encyclopaedia Britannica*, vol. 14 (1970), that 'the difference between magic and science lies in their basic premises'. The fact that this view is still current justifies the detail with which Englefield puts his arguments in this chapter (Eds.).

produce any particular effect we happen to desire. If one may
by administering a decoction of poppies induce sleep, and by
some other suitable prescription vomiting, dreams, intoxica-
tion, and even death, why should one not hope to find plants
capable of inducing forgetfulness, corporeal transformation,
the power of prophecy, or the passion of love? It is only from
our more exact knowledge of the active principles in plants
and their relation to human physiology that we are better able
to decide what is possible and what is not. In the absence of
such knowledge the sanguine expectation was not illogical.
It might be disappointed by experiment, but there are many
circumstances which may help to confirm a false belief once it
has been suggested, and to disguise the verdict of experiment.
Among the many symbolic shapes of flower or root there is no
lack of such as proclaim to the discerning seeker their fateful
virtues. And demand encourages supply. Even today it is
easier to claim powers for a new drug than to prove that they
are illusory.

In the same way astrology grew out of authentic
observations of a real correlation between celestial and terrestrial phenomena. Are not the positions of the stars connected
in an unmistakable manner with the changing seasons, the
coming of rain, the alternations of sun, of cold, of drought, or
of whatever may be the vital year-marks in the life of the
group? Every settled community needed a calendar and this
was only to be based on astronomical observations. The
connexion between the position of the stars, or of the sun in relation to the stars, and the significant terrestrial events which
they portended, was as obscure as that between the herb and
its medicinal efficacy. But if the stars determined the
succession of the seasons why should they not also determine
the other vital conditions of human prosperity, and perhaps
man's calamities as well? Not seeing the relation as the modern
astronomer sees it, is it not probable that the early stargazers
connected the aspect of the sky not with the seasons themselves
but with the practical effects of these on the community's
affairs? And as soon as this correlation between the stars and
human fortune had been recognized, fresh examples of similar
correlation would be easily discovered by a natural induction.
If a comet coincided with a calamity it would naturally receive

the blame. And as the responsibilities of the stars increased wise men would discover their secrets and not disdain the profits of divination.

Again, alchemy can be traced to *bona fide* chemical observations. Early metallurgical experiments and the distillation of plants and animal tissues would afford abundant material to build on. The extraction of metals from ore afforded ocular evidence of transmutation. The many observed cases of material transformation, the true conditions of which were quite unknown, would easily lead to the generalization that suitable manipulation by fire and other agencies could perhaps convert any material into any other. The needs and desires of men would accomplish the rest. In the absence of any sure guide as to what conditions and operations were relevant, especially if astrological conjunctions were taken into account, the number of experimental combinations was so great that the final discredit of alchemy was delayed until comparatively recent times.

So again with the various forms of augury and divination. If the stars had a hand in shaping the fortunes of mankind, so too had the clouds, the winds and the tides, the migrating birds, the swarming insects. The influence of such portents was manifest, its nature obscure. But the seers and prophets were there to furnish the true and authentic interpretation, and they had a good deal more to go upon than the vague generalization that all these things exerted some kind of influence. In many forms of divination the task of interpretation was akin to that of deciphering a hieroglyph. The gods were supposed to communicate their will and pleasure by means of signs, just as men do. And the divine signals were interpreted on similar principles. Such a belief could be derived only from experience of human communication and consisted in an extension to all kinds of natural forms and patterns—the intestinal convolutions of animals or the figures produced by flocks of birds in flight—of the signification truly attaching only to the ciphers and characters invented by man.

Today most of us are not so sure about the true nature of chemical affinity and the effects of medicines that we cannot sympathize with those who expected too much from such things. And yet we are all well aware that many relations have been clearly established. It is not difficult therefore to imagine such mistakes being made at a time when even the wise men knew very little. But when we come to those forms of magic which are based on primitive forms of communication the case is less clear. For here it is not so easy to see how misunderstanding could arise at all, how when once any form of communication had been invented its nature could be misunderstood. There are however examples of belief in the magical properties of writing which afford an intelligible illustration of the whole process, and by analogy with which we may reasonably attempt to reconstruct the earlier forms which are necessarily prehistoric.

Lane (1908, p.253) describes charms, common in the Egypt of his day, which consisted

> For the greater part, of certain passages of the Koran, and names of God, together with those of angels, genii, prophets, or eminent saints, intermixed with combinations of numerals, and with diagrams, all of which are supposed to have great secret virtues.

A similar practice was followed, according to Budge, by the ancient Egyptians, who carried amulets over which prayers and magical formulas were recited, or on which such words were inscribed (*Egyptian Magic*, p.26). The actual words were not necessarily understood by the owner of the amulet. In fact the less they were understood the easier it would be to credit them with superior virtue. There are cases recorded of scraps of printed books brought by travellers or missionaries, time-tables or dictionaries or bibles, treasured as potent charms by primitive folk. And there are many stories of men who knew nothing about writing, being astonished to observe the apparently magical properties of a few hieroglyphics drawn on a piece of paper. Now here we have the two stages in the usual process: first the observation of a real correlation the nature of which is not understood (the mysterious marks conveying an influence from their author to a stranger many miles away), and the second, the generalization by which all kinds of further powers are attributed to the same kind of agency. Since the characters are themselves meaningless to the uninitiated, he is ready to attribute the same power to any quaint markings that are unfamiliar to him, and as the nature of the power is unknown he assumes it to be much wider than it is.

This theory of the origin of written spells assumes that writing is already in existence and therefore that there are some at least who understand its nature; but it also assumes that there are others who understand nothing about it but are aware of its existence and have had some opportunity of witnessing what it can do. In this case we must assume the co-operation of men of superior and inferior knowledge. It may be that the observer of the stars understood their connexion with the seasonal changes as little as the most ignorant of his contemporaries, but the user of written symbols could not be so completely ignorant of the way in which they worked as those who credited them with supernatural powers. We have here, as an essential factor, a discrepancy of knowledge, since the observed correlation on which the false induction is based lies between a man-made instrument and its function. The watches of missionaries have in the same way often been credited with fanciful powers. The real powers are evident but, not being understood, cannot be accurately estimated. Errors resulting from such false attribution of powers are to be met everywhere and in every stage of culture, for it is a consequence of human inventiveness and curiosity and gains additional scope wherever invention runs in advance of the common understanding.

While, then, written charms can exist only among peoples who have made some acquaintance with writing, verbal magic is everywhere to be found, resting on the imaginary powers of spoken words. Here it is more difficult to conceive the state of mind in which such a belief can arise. One would perhaps suppose that every man who possessed the power of speech would understand the nature and the limits of the virtue of words. It might seem, at first sight, absurd to suggest that verbal magic could owe its origin to the same process as written magic. But there was surely once a time when conventional oral languages were a novelty and used only by initiates; magical beliefs about the power of these bizarre utterances having once originated could continue to be attached to special languages and formulas after a vulgar language had become widespread.

Where the language is intelligible its power may be of a less magical nature. Verbal magic is sometimes confounded with prayer and it is not easy to draw a distinction between them. Prayers are offered to gods or powerful spirits just as requests are made to fellow men. This involves nothing that is not involved in the normal use of language, even though the spirits are imaginary. But a magical formula does not express a wish or prayer, it exerts power. It cannot be improvised. It must have the correct form fixed by tradition or prescribed by the learned. It is not a speech that persuades but a spell that binds. Frazer (1919, p.104) points out that besides prayers addressed to the spirits of the dead for the purpose of procuring an abundant harvest, the wizards of certain tribes utter spells for the same purpose, and that these spells sometimes take the form, not of a command but of a narrative, addressed to nobody in particular, which the sorcerer mutters while he is performing his magical rites. Frazer conjectures that many ancient narratives, later regarded as mere myths, were at one time recited in magical rites for the purpose of actually producing events like those which they describe.

Now although our own highly cultivated languages always distinguish fairly clearly between statements and commands we cannot assume that primitive language was equally explicit. And if my theory is correct, the magical use of language might be expected to show traces of the fact that it originated when languages were new and crude. Language began as a mode of influencing others and whatever the shape of its early formulas it would at first be imperative in meaning. The compelling power of these formulas would lie not in the linguistic forms but in the physical and social relations between the parties. These conditions being assumed, the problem was merely to convey the idea of the action required. The imperative may be the primitive mood, but the more elaborate the command, the more would it assume the character of instructions and so involve what we now feel to be indicative or descriptive elements. General instructions of an impersonal character are even now often expressed in the indicative. 'Mr. X will lead the delegation; Mr. Y will arrange for hotel accommodation; Mr. Z will make arrangements with the travel agency.' Where the particular persons who are to be the subject of the command have to be mentioned, the third person is used, and in many languages there is no simple third person imperative. The proper use of the imperative is in addressing an individual, and in that case the name is not required. General commands and instructions are issued by persons in authority, and here in particular the need for names arises. The chief does not turn to each of his followers and slaves in turn and address them individually. He issues his commands impersonally so that all may hear. So-and-so will do this, and somebody else will do that. Such a command is a statement of what will take place and it is followed by its own fulfilment. This is the model of the magical use of words, not the verbal request expressed by one individual to his companion.

Names have always played an important part in magical procedure. And this is understandable, since if the verbal statement of an event can bring that event to pass, then the inclusion of a name in the statement will involve the owner of the name. Among the ancient Egyptians, according to Budge,

> It was believed that if a man knew the name of a god or a devil, and addressed him by it, he was bound to answer him and to do whatever he wished; and the possession of the knowledge of the name of a man enabled his neighbour to do him good or evil. . . . To the Egyptian the name was as much a part of a man's being as his soul, or his double (*ka*), or his body, and it is quite certain that this view was held by him in the earliest times. (*Egyptian Magic*, p. 157)

There was in consequence an understandable tendency for people, and also deities, to keep their real names secret.

The view that I have suggested, then, as applied to the particular case of verbal magic, is that the supposed efficacy of words for such purposes is the result of an unwarranted generalization from their observed real efficacy in special cases. At a time when oral language was still a novely employed perhaps only, like writing at a later date, by priests or magicians or chiefs and their associates or the initiates of secret societies, among the majority of the people the nature of the influence of words would not be understood. And indeed the real nature of this influence was by no means easy to understand and can hardly be said to be generally understood even today. Those who understood better might have motives for exploiting the misunderstanding of the others, and the weight of traditional belief would tend to suppress sceptical objections.

As the use of language became vulgarized, and its real limitations determined by experience, verbal magic would come to be restricted to archaic or unintelligible formulas handed down from ancient times, or formulas which owed some extraneous sanctity to their author or origin. Since there are no surviving peoples for whom language is not a fully familiar and universal accomplishment, we cannot look for recent magic formulations as in the case of writing. And what is true of conventional oral language is true still more evidently of the earlier language of signs or pantomime. We know of no people and have no record of any people still dependent on primitive pre-oral forms of communication, and so we cannot expect any direct evidence on the connexion between such communication and magical beliefs. Yet it is plain that the same principle can be applied in this case, and that just as written characters and spoken words could be credited with unreal powers, so gestures and pantomime may have been at an earlier time.

Lord Avebury quotes a passage from Plutarch's *Roman Questions* which compares primitive magic to the gesture-language. Nobody since Vico, Condillac and Warburton seems to have taken this hint, but none of these writers could have had enough knowledge of magical practices to appreciate the scope or the significance of this comparison.

By a movement of the arm one may direct the behaviour of a man. We beckon him and he comes, wave him away and he retires. These gestures are so habitual that we make them involuntarily even where they are necessarily ineffectual. We look at a man and he knows that we are thinking of him. The eyes are the focus of every facial expression, and reading a man's face is much the same as reading his eyes. Even animals when they look at you look at your eyes. And a facial expression can command obedience as much as a manual gesture or a word. Here we seem to have the grounds for two extensive types of magic, that which relies on a bodily movement such as beckoning, pointing or jumping (as when savages jump high in their ritual dances in order to encourage their crops to grow); and that associated with the Evil Eye. Where a simple gesture or facial expression does not suffice recourse is had to more elaborate pantomime, which may be supplemented by models, drawings, costumes and other properties. We have seen that these were the natural means of primitive communication, and it is not hard to show that every one of these forms reappears in the dramatic ritual of primitive magical and religious usage. Images and pictures have played the same part as names. The image of a being gives the owner of the image power over the original, just as knowledge of his name does to him who knows it. This belief played a large part in the practical witchcraft of Europe and examples are well known. Images of gods or powerful spirits are charms by which the services of those beings may be *commanded*. Models were used in what might almost be called a creative function. Budge tells (*Egyptian Magic*, p.67) that one of the officials of a king of the third dynasty received information that his wife was unfaithful to him. The co-respondent was accustomed at certain hours to bathe in the river, and so the husband made a wax model of a crocodile seven spans long, and then reciting certain magical words over it, he said: 'When the man cometh down to bathe in my waters seize thou him.' He then ordered his servant to cast the model into the water. The wax crocodile was duly transformed into the living reptile and the miserable paramour perished. In this case the image seems to have served as a means of summoning a creature into existence. The rod of Aaron which was changed into a serpent illustrates the same idea. The various creation legends in which the god moulds a man's image in mud or clay and breathes life into it have the same foundation. The mere construction and presentation of an effigy, like the utterance of a name, constitute a summons not to be resisted. Whether the being thus summoned is merely supposed to emerge from retirement, or to be called up from some limbo, or actually created out of nothing, may be a matter of uncertainty, and perhaps the distinction is not always clear in the mind of the magician. But the relation between such methods and pictorial methods of communication is fairly obvious. The real effect of an image or model is only to evoke an idea in the mind of the observer, just as the real effect of a name is only in the mind of the hearer. But the indirect effects of awakening an idea in another mind, and perhaps in many minds, are more notable than the invisible nervous disturbance. And these effects come to be attributed directly to the tangible cause, the name, the image, the model, and on the ground of such attribution the whole magical edifice is erected.

There are other ways of suggesting a man or an object besides names and images. Associated objects or actions of all kinds may serve the same purpose, as we have seen. And there is again no difficulty in pointing to common magical practices which employ the same method. Anything which suggests the idea of a man or object to observers may have the same wide-ranging effects as the presentation of an image or the mention of a name. And what at first could only serve for communication between companions became in time more generally intelligible, and the remoter consequences of any communication would be more difficult to trace. It is all very well to say, as is sometimes said in accounts of this kind of 'contagious' magic, that the associated object is felt to be a part of the man and is confounded with him. But this, even if sometimes true, cannot be accepted as natural or inevitable. If it is possible to influence a man by operating on his nail-parings, a lock of his hair, his clothes or any other possessions, there must be some connexion to account for the transfer effect. But to say that the man and his clothes are held to be one and the same is to explain a strange belief by one still stranger. Had such confusion been possible, not to say normal, it must have led, not to the small number of irrational practices which are resorted to on special occasions, but to universal chaos and insanity.

In the chapter on the improvised gesture-language I have attempted a classification of methods, and each of my categories can be matched with a type of magical practice illustrated by numerous examples in the collections of Tylor and Frazer. The chief categories enumerated in Chapter 6 were:

1. Emotional cries and facial expressions.
2. Demonstrative gestures such as pointing to or touching an object.
3. Dramatic gestures or pantomime, or acting the idea to be represented.

4. Plastic representation, making a model or figure or a simple dummy.
5. Graphic representation in two dimensions, drawing on the ground or in the air etc.

As a rule there was a mixture of more than one type, but I think any kind of natural or self-explanatory gesture must fall into one or other of these categories. As for the corresponding forms of magic, I have already given examples of 'plastic' magic. Graphic magic is represented by numerous examples of drawings of supposed magical potency with which weapons, tools, utensils and clothes are adorned. Emotional cries and facial expression—the latter often enhanced by paint—play a prominent part in magical rituals. The most important of all these categories, perhaps, is the third, and it is here that the analogies between primitive methods of communication, as illustrated above in Chapter 6, and magical ritual are the most striking. To express the idea 'high' one boy jumped in the air, another climbed on to a chair and reached up with his hands; another pretended to throw a ball into the air and watched its imaginary flight, shading his eyes with his hands. We are reminded of the magical practices employed to encourage growth, such as jumping for the crops. To express the ideas 'worm', 'crocodile', 'fish', several boys tried to represent the animals by squirming on the ground in a manner that recalls the totem dances. To express the idea 'life' or 'alive', two boys, quite independently, pretended to kill themselves or be killed; they fell to the ground and simulated death and then after a pause sprang up again as if suddenly restored to life. Does this not suggest the rite of killing the god and then making him come to life again in order to restore the life of the sun or of vegetation? When the seed is put into the ground it appears to die, and out of the dead body there seems to spring the new plant. 'That which thou sowest is not quickened except it die.' Paul saw in this a parallel to the resurrection. Can we not suppose that the same parallel had previously given rise to the magical process of pretending to raise a human being from the dead in order to produce a good harvest by encouraging the young plants to grow out of the dead seed?

These are examples of 'sympathetic' magic. Let us turn to those forms of magic called by Frazer 'contagious'. It was a frequent device, when an object having a characteristic colour was to be indicated, for a boy to point to any object of that colour. Further signs were of course needed to particularize the object. We may suppose that just as in speech the names of familiar objects came to be used as the names of colours, as rose, pink, violet, orange, etc., so the objects themselves would have been used for a similar purpose. On this simple and natural usage would then be based the belief that particular objects having a characteristic colour could be used to convey or impart a quality associated with that colour. Haddon writes (p 30):

> Certain stones from their colour suggested flesh; thus garnets and carnelians are worn in the rough or worked into beads as amulets against skin diseases.

And again, the Sem priest in the ceremony of mummification touched the mouth and eyes of the corpse

> . . . with a little bag filled with pieces of red stone or carnelian, with the idea, M. Maspero thinks, of restoring to the lips and eyelids the colour which they had lost during the process of mummification. (Budge, *Egyptian Magic*, p.197)

Other qualities, of course, besides colour can be denoted with the aid of particular objects—shape, texture, hardness and so on. And there is no lack of magical methods which involve the use of such objects to impart desired qualities. Sometimes a portion of an object was made to suggest the object as a whole, or a sample was made to serve a similar purpose. Thus water was indicated by moistening the finger or palm of the hand. To indicate tree one boy pointed to the wooden table. All kinds of symbolical methods were adopted, as when, to express 'rain' one boy pretended to put on a coat, another turned up his collar, a third pretended to put up an umbrella. With such methods may be compared the magical practices of sprinkling water to attract rain, of roaring to bring the thunderstorm, of whistling for the wind, and the use of phallic emblems and taboo.

Now it is not here suggested that every magical practice can be directly traced to some effective form of behaviour. Magical practices once established would breed. Whatever the

origin of a particular rite, that origin would eventually be forgotten even if it had ever really been understood. And such
rites would become the model for fresh ones having no direct
connexion with any kind of rational behaviour. What I do
suggest is that the whole of this vast accumulation of futile
practice, in spite of its non-adaptive character, can be
explained in terms of normal human psychology, in terms of
the same intellectual processes from which useful inventions
and scientific ideas have also come. There is no need to
suppose any peculiar primitive psychology, or to have recourse
to mystical theories. One still meets the idea that the behaviour
of men, especially primitive men, cannot really be explained
in terms of rational motives, that we must at all costs eschew
'intellectualist' interpretations. Since man, like all other
mammals, is essentially an intelligent animal, this self-denial
can only lead to vague or meaningless theories. Jane Harrison
wrote:

> Sympathetic Magic is, modern psychology teaches us, in
> the main and at the outset, not the outcome of intellectual
> illusion, not even the exercise of a 'mimetic instinct', but
> simply, in its ultimate analysis, an utterance, a discharge of
> emotion and longing. (p.34)

And again:

> The mimes are not mimicking thunder out of curiosity, they
> are making it and enacting it and uttering it for magical
> purposes. When a sailor wants a wind he makes it, or, as
> he later says, he whistles for it; when a savage or a Greek
> wants thunder to bring rain he makes it, becomes it. But it
> is easy to see that as the belief in magic declines, what was
> once intense desire, issuing in the making of or the being
> of a thing, becomes mere copying of it; the mime, the
> maker, sinks to be in our modern sense the mimic. (p.48)

But this kind of explanation does not explain. To say that in
using the bull-roarer or other magical device the medicine
man is making thunder, enacting thunder and uttering
thunder for magical purposes leaves us still wondering how he
should have come to suppose that he could make thunder in
that particular way. Alas, the expulsion of the intellectualist

devil has only made room for the seven devils of make-believe. For if we may not ascribe a man's behaviour to the rational choice of means, or his beliefs to any intelligible process of inference or hypothesis, what can we do but resort to occult principles?

CHAPTER 12

Thinking with Words

(i) The Quest for a Perfect Language

Thinking, however it may be conceived physiologically, consists essentially in doing in the imagination what one has first learnt to do with one's body, and in experiencing in the imagination what one has first experienced with one's senses (cf. above, p. 6). A man who is given to observation and contemplation will think pictorially. Those whose chief activity is talking or writing will think chiefly in words, for thinking in words is merely talking to oneself. Philosophers, who are mainly occupied with problems which do not lend themselves to practical experiment, are naturally prone to do most of their thinking with words. Plato seems to have accepted this as normal. In the *Theaetetus* Socrates says that by *conceiving* he means

> the conversation which the soul holds with herself in considering of anything. I speak of what I scarcely understand; but the soul when thinking appears to me to be just talking — asking questions of herself and answering them, affirming and denying. And when she has arrived at a decision, either gradually or by a sudden impulse, and has at last agreed, and does not doubt, this is called her opinion. I say, then, that to form an opinion is to speak, and opinion is a word spoken — I mean, to oneself and in silence, not aloud or to another . . . (Jowett, *Dialogues of Plato*, iv, p.252. Cf. also: *Sophist,* p.400, and *Philebus,* pp.609, 610)

More recently similar views have been expressed by behaviourists, although they replace the soul by the muscles involved in speech and writing. Watson, for instance (p.15) proposes that thought is merely speech, and that speech is essentially a form of muscular or glandular activity (cf. below, p.154).

If speech really were the sole content of mental activity, at least where rational thought is concerned, then it is natural that philosophers should conclude that right thinking might depend on establishing correct rules of grammar and syntax. Aristotle, in his logical treatises, seems to have been looking for such rules, and this search for rules of talking which would, if adhered to, guarantee correct conclusions continued throughout the Middle Ages. The Schoolmen, who were chiefly occupied with highly abstract ideas which did not lend themselves to visual or other sensory representation, had no reason to note the limitations of purely verbal thinking. But after the Renaissance, when philosophers became interested in the phenomena of the material world, and all kinds of things were discovered and investigated which had no names, thinking with non-verbal imagery became indispensable. Ordinary people, of course, had always thought in this way, as they still do; but it was the philosophers who speculated on the nature of the thinking process, and they only had their own experience to work on.

Descartes saw clearly that thinking involves something else besides words and that it is all too easy to substitute words for ideas (*Principes*, Part 1, No. 74). But whatever might be the real nature of the thinking process, it seemed to many that it could only be brought into the open, as it were, through language. We cannot observe another's thoughts but only listen to his words. For some reason it was not realized that a man's words were not the only key to his thoughts, even though every one knows that his thoughts are often more accurately revealed in his actions than in his words. Anyway, the recognition of the shortcomings of language stimulated practical minds to seek an improved medium, a philosophical language which by its very structure would preclude all fallacy and misunderstanding. During the seventeenth century mathematics had undergone a striking development which gave it more than ever the appearance of a powerful calculating machine. Logarithms were introduced by Napier in 1614, analytical geometry by Descartes in 1637, and the calculus by

Newton and Leibniz in the later part of the century. All these inventions were methods of manipulating the written symbols of algebra and arithmetic, so as to perform calculations which by older methods were either impossible or very laborious. If such miracles could be performed by the mere manipulation of letters and symbols, why should not something even better be possible with the apparently more complex forms of language? This seems to have been the idea which haunted Leibniz. Many attempts were made to invent a scientific language free from the defects of the languages in common use. But the aims of such innovators were not all the same. George Dalgarno and Bishop Wilkins were concerned chiefly with language as a universal means of communication and sought to systematize the relation between form and meaning. The theory in both cases was that all the various things that require names should first be classified according to a natural system, and names then assigned in such a way that the name of a thing could always be inferred from its place in the classi-fication and vice versa. The first task therefore was to cata-logue the universe. Wilkins, a founder-member of the Royal Society, undertook this without apparent misgiving. From Max Müller's account (II, 65) of this system, it is evident that such a language, however scientifically constructed, could only eliminate grammatical anomalies and systematize the vocabulary. It could not provide any remedy for those defects of language which give rise to misconceptions and fallacious reasoning. Constancy of grammatical form, modelled on familiar European types, cannot ensure any kind of logical consistency between propositions.

Leibniz, apparently, realized the limitations of Wilkins's system. In letters quoted by Dugald Stewart he proceeds to outline his own plan which was to treat the science of mind by a mathematical method and by inventing an art

> which, with an exactitude resembling that of a mechanism, may render the operations of reason steady and visible, and, in their effects on the minds of others, irresistible.

It seems that Leibniz thought he had invented, or that given time he would be able to invent, a system of symbols, a quasi-mathematical language, which would constitute an infallible calculus for ascertaining the truth on any conceivable subject.

The idea of a universal language based on logical principles occupied the minds of other sanguine philosophers in the seventeenth and eighteenth centuries. Venn refers to a number of authors and works proposing or constructing languages of this kind. Even in the nineteenth century there were still some who believed that it should be possible to devise a logical symbolism which would (in Leibniz's phrase) 'put it out of our power to commit an error'. These attempts seem to have been based on a common delusion that ordinary human language, however imperfect as a reasoning machine, was capable of *representing* the whole range of human ideas, and that therefore it was only necessary to find a way of combining the logical virtue of mathematical symbols with the comprehensiveness of normal language in order to have a machine which would solve all problems.

(ii) Some Nineteenth-Century Views

In the eighteenth century the ever increasing interest in anthropological questions led to much speculation on the origin of language, which inevitably raised again the problem of the relation of language to thought. If language was to be explained as an invention like the bow or the plough, then it seemed necessary to assume that men were already in possession of all their reasoning faculties before they had any means of communicating with one another. But if, as philosophers generally held, reasoning was impossible without language, then such an assumption was not permissible. That this difficulty was not really insuperable was recognized by Vico, Warburton, Condillac, Monboddo, Thomas Reid and others. But it was not easy to make the more orthodox understand that the development of the means of communication and of the reasoning powers were simultaneous processes which furthered one another mutually. This, after all, involved the notion of mental evolution. Writers of the eighteenth century were content to accept the processes of invention and imitation as obvious facts, and to rely on them for their explanations. In the nineteenth century these assumptions came to be doubted and attempts were made to do without them. But since invention and imitation are facts, the better course would have been to begin by studying them, and to find out when and where they occur, so as to ascertain how far it is justifiable to use them as explanatory principles. But the conclusion of Rousseau: — 'La parole paraît avoir été fort nécessaire 'pour établir l'usage de la parole' — was generally accepted in the nineteenth century as finally excluding all theories of invention. Language was either the gift of God, or, according to the evolutionists, had developed in the same way as all the other specifically human characters. And both the evolutionists and the believers in a divine gift were agreed that language was either the same thing as the reason or was so closely related to it that the two could not be separated or distinguished. F. Schlegel, for instance, described man's reception of the divine gift of language as 'a dawning of the inward feeling':

> Where the feeling for truth is once there, words and signs easily find themselves without any other aid, and the deeper and more intense the feeling, the nobler and more significant will they be (p.106)

Wilhelm von Humboldt held that

> Language could not be invented if its archetype were not already present in the human understanding. ... If, therefore, that to which there is really nothing analogous in the whole realm of the thinkable may be compared to anything, then we can only recall the natural instinct of animals, and call language an intellectual instinct of the reason. (p.248)

Whatever we may think of their arguments, when we can understand them, it cannot be denied that the German philosophers and philologists of the nineteenth century did something by their example to show the important part that may be played in thought by mere words. Max Müller, who strongly maintained that without speech there can be no reason, cites both Schelling and Hegel in his support. From Hegel he merely quotes: 'It is in names that we think.' But Hegel did on one occasion express himself more at length on the subject of language, and as the passage is a perfect example of thinking with words I venture to translate it. It occurs in the *Phänomenologie des Geistes* (Section 6, p.330), a book which, it is said, he wrote to the sound of the guns at the battle of Jena. If this is true it may be regarded as an extenuating circumstance. I cannot give any account of the context except that it is in very much the same vein:

(Language as the Reality of Alienation or Culture).
This alienation (*Entfremdung*), however, only happens in language, which here appears in its peculiar significance. — In the world of morality, law and commandment, in the world of reality merely advice, it (i.e. language) has Being for its Content and is the Form of the latter: but here it receives the Form, which it itself is, as Content, and is valid as Speech; it is the power of language as such which performs what is to be performed. For it is the existence of the pure self, as self; in it the self-existent singularity of the Self-consciousness as such comes into existence, so that it exists for others. The Ego, as this pure Ego, is otherwise not there; in every other utterance it is absorbed into a reality, and in a form, from which it can withdraw; it is reflected back into itself by its activity and by its physiognomical expression, and leaves such imperfect existence, in which there is always as much too much as too little, lying lifeless. But language contains it in its purity, it alone expresses the Ego, the Ego itself. This, its existence, is, as Existence, a Subjectivity which has in it its true nature. The Ego is this Ego — but likewise universal; its appearing is just as immediately the alienation and the disappearance of this Ego, and consequently its persistence in its universality. The Ego which expresses itself is heard; it is a contagion, in which it has passed over directly into unity with those for whom it is there, and is universal self-consciousness. — By being heard its existence itself has at once become extinct; this its Otherness is reabsorbed into itself, and this precisely is its Being, as self-conscious Now, while being there not to be there, and to be there by ceasing to exist. This disappearance is, therefore, itself directly its persistence; it is its own Knowledge of itself, and its Knowledge of itself as one which has passed over into another self, which has been heard, and which is universal.

The reader may suppose that my translation does not do him

justice. I have kept as close to the original as possible. The truth is, of course, that where so many words of quite uncertain meaning are strung together, however impeccable the grammar and the syntax, interpretation is out of the question. The meaning of a word is always largely dependent on the context, and where the whole context is equally indeterminate, the meaning of the writer, if there is one, must remain inaccessible.

Why did Hegel write in this way? Perhaps the most plausible explanation is that he wished to be regarded as a profound thinker, as one who saw more deeply into the nature of things than other men. This is the traditional role of the religious leader, the seer, the prophet. And Hegel's language is, accordingly, dark and enigmatic. Today the man of science has usurped much of the prestige formerly enjoyed by the prophet, and in order to win the same respect the ambitious writer today must assume the style and mannerisms of the scientist. Even though he has no observations to report, or new interpretations of previous observations, it is possible, by the invention of a strange jargon, preferably involving the use of unfamiliar symbols, and by writing in a convoluted, seemingly meticulous, prose style, to convince many readers that he has invented a new science.

(iii) The Real Usefulness of Words

If it is asked why so many philosophers from Plato onwards have wrongly supposed that the process of thinking was essentially a process of talking to oneself, the answer is, I think, that words do in fact play an important part in thought, especially abstract thought. Words serve a real function in the reflective process—not as a logical mechanism, but as mnemonics and as summaries.

Words become associated with things, but they also become associated with one another. Partly by their sound but chiefly by the muscular movements by which we utter them, words become linked together. We can learn to pronounce long sequences of words, thousands at a time. They need not be visualized. They are committed to the muscular memory and can be repeated in the correct order as often as we like. Most men have a considerable memory for verbal sequences, and some are thus gifted to an extraordinary degree.

Now since words are also associated with ideas and things, this recording of word sequences in the memory has a valuable mnemonic function. Ideas are also linked in the memory and one idea recalls another. But ideas have multiple associations and are always highly composite. To establish a one-dimensional chain of ideas in the memory would mean annulling all lateral linkages, and each component idea would have to be reduced to some brief and restricted representative element. In fact, when we allow our memory to be freely active the sequence of associated ideas is never the same. It is this apparently random ebb and flow of thoughts which is the source of all novelty and invention. But when experiment has taught us how to achieve our aim in any particular situation we need to remember how the thing was done. It may be that a long succession of actions was involved, performed in a definite order. If the sequence can be repeated often enough for a habit to be formed there will be no further need for reflexion. But a complicated operation may consist in a sequence of actions each one of which will vary to some extent according to the particular circumstances. It is the sequence of actions that has to be remembered, not the exact sequence of movements. The component actions may be represented by words, and the words committed to memory in the required order. Such verbal *directions* for carrying out a great number of complex operations are retained in the memory and can be referred to when required.

This seems to be the true function of language in thought. Experience has taught us to combine certain acts or to expect certain sequences or combinations of events. If these combinations or sequences are not too extensive we may remember them in a more direct way. But where they involve too many components we find it easier to represent the latter by words and link the words in our memory. The verbal formulas thus recorded can be recalled by merely initiating the sequence of words. We recall the first phrase and then the rest is revived automatically. With its aid the whole complex of acts or events or circumstances is reconstructed in the imagination. Linguistic formulas, then, serve for indexing purposes. The final results of complex operations with material objects can be recorded in the memory as statements, or maxims, such as 'acid corrodes metals', 'horses eat oats', or 'sugar dissolves in water'. Such phrases recall a whole series of remembered experiments and serve to link them in the memory.

These remembered word-sequences are merely a machinery for the more systematic organization of the memory. They represent the things with which they are associated only in that they are able to revive the *thoughts* of them in the memory. We cannot, except perhaps in a few simple cases, experiment with the words as we can with the visual, tactile and auditory images. If the latter are but an imperfect substitute for the real things, the words are an even more imperfect substitute for these images. In simple and concrete cases reasoning may be carried on for a short time by verbal formula. Where the facts are familiar and the correlations well known we may get to rely on verbal expressions without any recall of tangible experiences. From the bare statement in the news bulletin that it is going to rain we may decide on an appropriate course of action without any mental representation of streaming windows or puddles and mud. From the verbal announcement of a particular event we may jump directly to the verbal statement of the probable consequence without the mediation of any concrete imagery. But this sort of verbal reasoning can only be valid where the linkage is familiar and habitual. There is no safeguard against false inference in the nature of the words themselves or their sequence. It is therefore only in the realm of customary events and well established correlations among familiar things that inferences from verbal formulas, unsupported by any reference, either external or imaginative, to concrete realities, are not precarious.

CHAPTER 13

Some recent views on Language

[The material of the preceding twelve chapters formed part of Englefield's original book. We, as editors, have merely abridged and in some cases rearranged the order of the material, and added in footnotes references to some recent relevant discussion. In the chapter that follows, we have assembled material from Englefield's notebooks and commentaries on some recent writings on language. Although all the authors concerned are well known and widely quoted, it will be seen that they are not treated with great respect. It may be that Englefield selected for scrutiny their most inept or foolish passages; but this does not matter. It is the ideas, not the authors, which are under attack. The existence in print of these passages emphasizes the present need for a sober reasonable approach to a subject so littered with bizarre theories. Englefield's criticisms of these authors are based on principles which are enumerated, sometimes at considerable length, in the preceding chapters. The apparent obviousness of these principles is due to their being lucidly stated. It will be clear from what follows that, however obvious, they are not universally recognized (Eds.)]

(i) The Problem of Origins

(a) *Diamond*

In his *The History and Origin of Language,* A.S. Diamond tries to solve the problem of origins by extrapolation from existing languages. He distinguishes three types of sentence:

      1. Look!   2. George runs.   3. George is fast.

This sequence, he says, is the order of simplicity and primitiveness, and is marked by a 'decrease in the proportion of verbs'. By 'verb' he means a word which signifies an action or movement (p.17), although it is surely obvious that this is often not true of verbs in the dictionary sense, while on the other hand there are innumerable nouns and adjectives which also signify action or movement. Comparing the vocabularies of English of different periods, he finds that the verbs preponderate in the earlier and that the proportion of nouns and adjectives increases with the later periods. And he attempts a much wider induction. He distinguishes stages of social progress through which humanity has passed in the last million years or so, from subsistence by food gathering in the Old Stone Age, to hunting and later to agriculture, and so on. He then picks out from existing tribes, or tribes which have existed recently enough to be studied, those which he regards as representative of each of these successive stages; and he finds, on studying their languages, that the more primitive stages have a preponderance of verbs, and that the proportion of nouns and adjectives increases in the later stages. For instance, he takes two North American tribes as representative of the civilization of the Stone Age and supposes that their language enables him to make inferences about the language of their ancestors several hundred thousand years ago.

This whole procedure is open to obvious objections. Every action involves some body or part of a body, and it may be as easily indicated by reference to the part as to the movement. Even if in any particular case it is found that the earliest recorded form of a word is a verb, this proves only that the verb was used a few hundred years ago; but we still have to ask where it came from, and there is no reason at all for asserting that it must have been a verb from palaeolithic times. Man may have been speaking for perhaps a hundred thousand years, and extrapolation over such a period from the tiny portion of time of which we have exact knowledge is fantastic. There is no ground at all for supposing that the changes which we observe in the latest epoch have been continuing since the beginning.

Furthermore, Diamond's allegations about the relative frequency of verbs and nouns are not true of the languages of some uncivilized peoples, even though he writes about 'all the languages of the world' (e.g. pp.113, 117). For instance, he assumes that the Sakai and Semang of Malaya are among the modern tribes who represent the men of the Old Stone Age, and he says that there is insufficient evidence to determine the proportions of the parts of speech in their language. This is a remarkable statement, since in 1906 Skeat and Blagden published a comparative vocabulary of the aboriginal dialects of Malaya of over 250 pages. The number of English words to which the two authors give native equivalents is between four and five thousand, and this compares favourably with many of the vocabularies Diamond uses. The evidence of Skeat and Blagden certainly does not support his theory. For instance, taking 36 consecutive pages of their vocabulary, I have counted 53 verbs, 167 nouns and 31 adjectives. These figures reckon 'blowpipe' as one noun, although in fact 18 different nouns are given for the parts of this important weapon. That these peoples had plenty of occasion for the use of nouns is also clear from the numerous plant names in the list, and the inclusion of many anatomical features (brow, eyebrow, breath, etc.).

Diamond asserts that in all known languages 'the shortest and simplest form of the verb is the request for action, the second person singular of the imperative' (p.111). In fact this is not true of Arabic, where the imperative is formed by prefixing a letter to the third person singular of the aorist. I cannot speak for all the other languages of the world. Nevertheless, there are certainly many where the imperative consists of the verbal root reduced to a minimum. It does not follow that this is 'the earliest and most primitive form of the verb' (p.121). It may be that the frequency of use brings about a reduction, as it does in so many other cases. (Diamond himself notes that, in some languages, the imperative is actually reduced (p.113), and he is not unaware (p.136) that forms which are very common tend, for that reason, to become brief and simple.)

Diamond believes that the infinitive is brief like the imperative, and he infers a close relation between the two. Again, he purports to be speaking of all the languages of the world, although in fact there is no infinitive in Arabic. A weak point about this book is the author's unquestioning reliance on all the old grammatical conventions of Latin. His theory seems to be that the first words used were verbs in the imperative, and that later man learned to make simple statements (like 'George runs') by first turning this imperative into an infinitive or verbal noun, and then adding a pronoun ('his running').

The distinction between imperative and indicative communication is not so great as Diamond imagines. Descriptions are an indispensable part of any request for a detailed action. Even the simplest imperative communication, in so far as it indicates the *kind* of action that is requested, must in some way *describe* that action. When Sarah wants me to throw her stick, she brings it and lays it on the ground in front of me. Her action requests an action on my part and also contains an indication of the kind of action required from me. If she wants to go out into the garden she stands by the door and whimpers. The request is obvious and may be called an imperative, but it also indicates what I am requested to do.

In any case, the grammatical distinctions invoked by Diamond are quite inapplicable to primitive language. Cultural development occurs as a process of differentiation, and the earliest signs — whether words or gestures or pictures — can surely be regarded neither as verbs or nouns or adjectives. The same sign would, according to our notions, serve each purpose in turn. This is obvious in Ancient Egyptian, and even in Malay or English. Diamond does not hesitate to analyse the words of any language into the conventional eight parts of speech. This can always be done if the words in question can only be made to correspond to some English word whose grammatical category is known from the English dictionary. If the Malay word *hidup* means 'to live', then it is a verb, and if we then find that it also means 'life', we have to say that there is another word, having the same form, which is a noun. If the Englishman says 'Away with him!' or 'Out of it!' we do not say that 'away' and 'out' are imperative verbs, but that these are abridged expressions in which a verb is 'understood'. Yet it is clear that these words may be assimilated to the verbal scheme, and we may say that he was 'outed'. The early verbs of a language which we cannot trace further back may very well in the same way be derived from prepositions or adverbs or nouns or adjectives.

But in the primitive stage of language, when — I have

argued — gesture made up its essential framework, it is just as likely that the first words represented things or states as events. The whole theory of Diamond rests on the assumption that language began as speech and that the earliest words were also the earliest mode of communication. For otherwise, the change from imperative to indicative would have been accomplished before language (i.e. speech) began.

Diamond, then, thinks that language originated in requests for action, made by one man to another. (From the fact that, where a distinction exists between the masculine and feminine gender, it is always the former that is the primitive form, he deduces (p.144) that the primitive request for action was always addressed to males!) He further argues that, because a man would naturally ask help in doing something that he was not strong enough to do himself, it follows that the first requests he would make would be actions which smashed or killed something — 'actions requiring the maxium of bodily effort . . . Break it! Kill it!' (p.145). Furthermore, in order that the request and its effect might be obvious to all bystanders so that they might learn the form of words, both verbal expression and result must be noisy and conspicuous (pp.156, 157). Now it can hardly be argued that the earliest manipulations of men were always of this violent nature, for apes are capable of performing all kinds of non-violent and skilful operations. Diamond's point must therefore be that the only requests which would become attached to a verbal utterance and therefore originate language were those which called attention to themselves by their conspicuous and violent effects. The difficulty which he is here trying to overcome is the communal nature of language. It is not enough for two individuals to discover a way of conveying to one another their requests. If a language is to develop the same methods must be used by all. Hence the method adopted by Henry when addressing Tom must be such as to attract the attention of the rest of the community. If we imagine, for example, one man requesting another to fix two bamboos together for him, in the manner of Köhler's ape (cf. above, p.8n.), then it is only too likely that the conversation might be entirely overlooked by everybody else, and the word invented for the purpose would never become part of the common vocabulary, though it might continue in use between the two individual men. Diamond does not envisage the possibility of a deliberate convention in his discussion of this problem. His theory, then, is that men began to speak by making involuntary utterances when they sought help from their fellows in order to accomplish some violent action. Their own state of mind would be highly excited, and the excitement would be transmitted to the person addressed. The involuntary utterance would come to be recognized as the sign for the violent action called for. Onlookers would be deeply impressed, and the appeal as well as the response would remain in their memory, so that in time all the members of the community would get to recognize the connexion between the cries of appeal and the violent responsive action (p.158). In due course, all alike would learn to make similar appeals and to respond to them by the same violent actions. Thus the first words were such as are uttered in the process of making a violent action, and these came to be the names for the actions in question.

These cries of appeal were originally accompanied, says Diamond, by frantic gestures, but after a few millennia the excitement abated, and people gradually left out the gestures and only made the noises. While discussing the role of gesture in primitive language he speaks of the 'tearing, smashing, demolishing tendencies' of apes and children, and supposes that this supports his theory. But any reader of Köhler's book will see how misleading this is. Pulling a thing to pieces to make closer acquaintance with it is not usually a violent operation. Animals and unskilful people destroy the objects they examine as a result of experiment and trial and error. Anybody who in complete ignorance of the structure of a clock tries to take it to pieces to see how it works is likely to end by destroying it, even though he may have been very gentle in all his actions. But for Diamond's theory it is not enough that the action should merely result in destruction; it must be violent, vigorous, massive, noisy, so as to attract attention, and it must require the exertion of more strength than most ordinary individuals possess, since that is why they make the request for help. We see here a fallacy in the argument based on the ambiguity of the word 'destruction'. In one part of the argument it is made to imply violence and in another merely an action which results in the disintegration of any object.

Diamond argues that animals gesticulate under the stress of emotion, that they are most strongly affected by emotion when they call for assistance and require a violent action to be performed on their behalf. Under these emotional conditions they make frantic movements and utter cries, and this leads to helpful action on the part of another animal — action which is generally similar in character to the frantic movements by which it is summoned. He seems to suppose that the gestures of apes are necessarily violent contortions of the whole body and prompted only by strong emotion. Thus he quotes Köhler's account of the chimpanzee's manner of acting under tense emotion (pp.158, 318), but overlooks the fact that this animal is just as capable of quiet gesture as he is of this uncoordinated and violent expression of emotion. Even Dinah and Sarah, who are mere dogs, can express their wishes by gestures which involve no more than a movement of the paw or muzzle, or even of the eyes. (At this moment I heard a very gentle 'whoof' outside my door. It was Sarah asking whether it was not dinner time.)

Finally, the request for action, which Diamond makes his starting point in tracing the origin of language, is not needed at all. If two or more individuals desire the same result, they will naturally both work for it. And if it is a case where they can do more when they combine their efforts, there is no reason why they should not discover this. Every piece of learnt behaviour which serves a purpose must first occur spontaneously, or for some other purpose previously learned. The animal can learn that a particular kind of behaviour will achieve a particular result only if he first performs the action and *discovers* its effect. If animals learn the value of co-operation, it must be because in some circumstances they find themselves co-operating and are rewarded. The action which is in the event rewarded is not performed in the first case for the sake of the reward. It must therefore be performed for some other reason: either for some other *purpose,* or merely as the result of a combination of circumstances. In the present case there is no great difficulty. If a number of individuals having the same purpose act simultaneously in the same situation and turn out by doing so to achieve their common end more effectually than any one of them could have done alone, then there is the situation in which they may learn to co-operate. Thus do wolves learn to co-operate in pursuing a prey too powerful for one of them. Communication began, I have suggested, when animals discovered by trial and error, even by chance, that by making certain movements or sounds, or by adopting certain attitudes, they influenced their fellows in a desirable way.

(b) *Revesz*

Revesz's *Ursprung und Vorgeschichte der Sprache* was published in 1946 and an English translation appeared in 1956. He believes that the gulf between human language and animal noises cannot be bridged, but nevertheless sees no reason for abandoning 'the idea of a continuously or discontinuously progressive development in biological occurrences' (p.13). He therefore gives his attention to the principle of development and looks to see if any expressions or tendencies are to be found in recent man which point to a pre-speech stage (*vorsprachliche Stufe*) or archaic form, and can be taken as a starting point for an 'evolutionary theory of language'. He seems to feel that the great merit of his theory is that it reconciles the basic requirements of evolution theory with a proper conception of the dignity and uniqueness of human language. It is no longer possible to deny that man and all his works are the result of an evolutionary process. But, thanks to the modern techniques of philosophical exegesis, it is possible to show that this does not involve the humiliating consequences once supposed to flow from it.

What separates man from the animals, according to Revesz, is his reason *(Vernunft)* and 'an unambiguous sign of the presence of reason is language' (p.18). He adds: 'Without language, no man; without man, no language'. This maxim is illustrated by a fanciful passage discussing the logical dilemma of an anthropologist faced either with a speechless creature physically resembling a man or with a talking monkey. The problem, apparently, is to be resolved by a taxonomic system based on verbal distinctions. Revesz seems to think that because it is convenient to have a definition, the most convenient definition is a revelation of the truth. But as quite a number of men, not to mention children, cannot speak, this particular definition is hardly a satisfactory one.

Revesz argues that if speech is regarded as the principal characteristic of man, if man and speech are inseparably united, the hypothesis of a speechless man has no sense. This, no doubt, is logically unanswerable. But that does not make it sensible. If we believe that man had some speechless ancestor, it really is of no importance whatever whether we call such an ancestor 'man' or 'preman' or 'protoman' or 'eoman' or anything else. What is of importance is that we should be able to form some idea of what he was like and what his psychological endowments were and how he could in course of time develop into the kind of man we meet today.

We come now to the 'concept of origin' (p.21). Revesz says that, by the origin of any phenomenon or function, we may mean the protoform *(Urform)* in which it first occurred, or its pre-stages *(Vorstufen)*. The pre-stages of a statue, for instance, would consist in the raw material, whereas 'the first rough moulding, which already partly reveals the intention of the sculptor . . . is already the protoform of the completed work'. On the strength of this analysis of the concept of origin he divides the history of language into three phases:

(1) The *prehistory (Vorgeschichte)* which includes the stages of preparation for speech, i.e. its pre-stages *(Vorstufen)*.
(2) The *early history (Frühgeschichte)* which tries to reconstruct the early stages *(Frühstufen)* of language out of the beginnings of sound- and gesture-language.
(3) The true *history of language* 'which describes the historical development of the speech system we know'.

Thus we have *Vorgeschichte, Frühgeschichte* and *Sprachgeschichte.* The *Vorgeschichte* includes the *Vorstufen,* the *Frühgeschichte* the *Frühstufen.* He does not say, but perhaps we may assume, that the *Sprachgeschichte* includes the *Sprachstufen.* He ends this analysis by claiming that 'this evolutionary classification gives the basis of a *phase-theory*' (p.22).

Revesz devotes a surprising amount of space to demonstrating the obvious fact that emotional noises are different from the sounds of articulate speech. Language, he says, is deliberate, and the emotional expression is instinctive. The latter 'lacks all generic community with speech' and so 'cannot be regarded either as early form (*Frühform*) or as pre-form (*Vorform*) of speech' (p.40). 'One can accept the calls of animals at most as *Vorstufe*, but not as *Frühstufe* of language' (p.23). They 'originate in a different need and pursue a different goal, and consequently have nothing to do with the endeavour which finds vent in speech' (p.49). It is quite clear that he accepts as a fundamental principle that no form of behaviour can ever arise from another form which served a different purpose. Why he should believe this is not clear. Evolutionary history abounds with instances of bodily parts—the bat's wing, for instance, or the ossicles of the middle ear—which have undergone a complete change from their original function. I have endeavoured to show, in an earlier section of this book, that analogous transformations occur, and are important, in the sphere of behaviour.

Revesz insists on the great importance of 'exact discrimination between *Vorstufe* and *Frühstufe*' (p.23). This would be reasonable if he were assuming a sequence of evolutionary stages and demanding that the different stages in the development of language should be assigned to their appropriate stage. For example, suppose that we could distinguish three stages in human evolution, characterized by a certain mental capacity: eo-homo, proto-homo and pre-homo. Then in reconstructing the process by which various human inventions were made or institutions originated, we should have to know first of all in which era they occurred. If, for example, the first use of pictographs occurred in the time of proto-homo, then we must not, in our explanation of the occurrence, assume any human capacity or proclivity to be found only in pre-homo. Unfortunately we have at present no means of distinguishing such evolutionary stages and must do our best without any precise knowledge. Revesz's discussion of pre-forms, proto-forms and so on is little more than a juggling with definitions, bearing no relation to experience or to established facts. It does not in the smallest degree explain or make clearer the origin or the prehistory of language.

(ii) Chomsky and Linguistics[1]

Noam Chomsky is well known as a pioneer of the modern 'science' of linguistics. His writings are far from lucid, but one may charitably attribute their obscurity to the technicalities of his method. From a reading of three of his longer works, it emerges that Chomsky's main concern is with grammar. He maintains that we cannot speak correctly without a grasp of the rules of grammar. But as the child appears to learn to speak without having instruction in these rules, he must — so Chomsky argues — inherit an unconscious knowledge of them. In other words, they are innate, not learned by induction. Furthermore, since the child can learn any language as easily as any other, there must be rules that are common to all languages. The grammatical conventions of English are different from those of French, but a child of English parents brought up in France has no difficulty in learning French. So there must be some deep underlying rules common to all languages, and knowledge of these rules is innate. Chomsky admits that these rules have not yet been discovered, but he clearly supposes that the quest for them will throw light on the human mind. What is common to every individual human mind is something that vitally concerns the psychologist. This is why 'linguistics' is of such great importance, why it may revolutionize psychological thinking, and even affect our view of the fundamentals of all science!

Chomsky calls the universal rules 'universal grammar'. Although he cannot say exactly wherein this consists, he does think that he can get near to it by distinguishing what he calls a 'deep structure' underlying the surface of ordinary speech. His idea seems to be that the deep structure of a sentence represents an analysis into a series of propositions. He believes that

> a system of propositions expressing the meaning of a sentence is produced in the mind as the sentence is realized as a physical signal, the two being related by certain formal operations that, in current terminology, we may call *grammatical transformations* (*Language and Mind*, p.25)

1.   The author has discussed this subject in greater detail in *Trivium*, 9 (1974) (Eds.).

He supposes that when we hear the sentence 'a wise man is honest', we can understand it only by analysing it into two propositions: 'a man is wise' and 'a man is honest'. These two propositions represent the deep structure of the sentence. Chomsky, then, supposes that if an adjective is attached to a noun in a sentence, the speaker must mentally conceive the noun as the subject of a proposition in which the adjective is the predicate. Thus, if I say 'white elephants are rare', this means that I think to myself: 'elephants are white', 'elephants are rare'. In point of fact I think neither of these things.

Chomsky is so obsessed with the importance of grammar that he attributes grammatical conventions to the processes of thought itself. But, as I have tried to make plain (above, pp.98-9), vocabulary is far more important than grammar. One can make oneself understood with the aid of quite ungrammatical sentences, so long as the right words are used; otherwise we should never understand a foreigner who spoke our language incorrectly. On the other hand, correct grammar will not make a statement intelligible unless the vocabulary is so. The important thing about a word is its meaning, that is to say what it denotes. Chomsky's writings are grammatically correct; his sentences contain subject, verb and predicate; but to me they are often unintelligible because of their vocabulary. For the purposes of everyday intercourse among acquaintances, when one is referring to matters of common interest, and when one can assume the existence of a large field of common knowledge, modes of expression which might otherwise seem ambiguous or obscure are made readily intelligible by the context. Ideas represent things and events in the real world, and our words are used to represent the same things and events. Such a sentence as 'Old What's-his-name has done it again' could represent a perfectly clear idea in the mind of the speaker and convey an equally clear idea to the listener, though of course in the witness box, before a judge and a jury, it might have to be expanded into a whole paragraph. What Chomsky calls the 'surface structure' is made intelligible by the common knowledge of the persons communicating, and by their common vocabulary, and certainly not by some theoretical grammatical expansion performed in the mind of the listener, which would in any case be impossible

if he had not already divined the meaning. Chomsky, however, insists that it is the 'deep structure' of a sentence that
enables us to understand it. This deep structure, he says, is
'the underlying abstract structure' that 'determines the
semantic interpretation' (i.e. the meaning) of the sentence.
He adds: 'Of course, this deep structure is implicit only; it is
not expressed but is only represented in the mind' (*Cartesian
Linguistics*, pp.33, 34). One naturally asks how it is represented in the mind—as a verbal proposition, or as some kind
of an image or series of images? Chomsky's implication is that
it is represented as a verbal sequence—more elaborate than
the surface structure, but still merely a sequence of words. He
does not expressly commit himself to this view that thinking is
merely talking to oneself, but he certainly implies it. And his
motive for so doing is clear. He wants to convey the idea that
the psychology of thinking is essentially the concern of linguistics. He says (p.35):

> The deep structure that expresses the meaning is common
> to all languages, so it is claimed [it is clear from the context
> that Chomsky endorses the claim], being a simple reflection
> of the forms of thought.

What, then, are the forms of thought? And if a 'simple reflec-
tion' of them is a grammatical structure, what else—on this
view—can thought be except some kind of language?

Not surprisingly, there are cases in which Chomsky finds it
hard to supply a satisfactory 'deep structure' of the form
indicated above, where every part has to be presented in the
form of propositions consisting of subject, verb and predicate.
An example is the sentence 'John was persuaded to leave'.
However, he manages to construct the deep structure underlying this by analysing it into: (1) 'John leave', and (2) 'persuade John', where John is understood to be the subject of
'leave' and the object of 'persuade'. He says:

> Although the deep structure must be constituted of such
> propositions, if the approach . . . outlined earlier is correct,
> there is no trace of them in the surface structure of the
> utterance. The various transformations that produce [the
> sentence 'John was persuaded to leave'] have thoroughly

obliterated the system of grammatical relations and functions that determine the meaning of the sentence. (*Language and Mind*, p.31)

We see, then, that the person who made the statement 'John
was persuaded to leave' had in his mind a deep grammatical
structure, no trace of which remains in his utterance. But for
this deep grammatical structure the utterance would be
meaningless, for the deep structure 'determines the meaning
of the sentence'. Chomsky does not often mention the 'meaning' and usually prefers some camouflage expression, such as
'the semantic interpretation' of the sentence. He certainly
supposes that we only arrive at the meaning through the deep
structure, but he is unable to indicate how the two are related.
He says that 'the deep structure expresses those grammatical
functions that play a role in determining the semantic interpretation' (p.26), but he cannot indicate what this role is, nor
how it is played. What is clear is that his theory of deep and
surface structure implies that all ideas and thoughts must take
the form of propositions, grammatically constructed with
subject and verb. A sentence heard must first be 'transformed'
into this form in order to be understood, and a thought must
first be transformed from this deep grammatical form, in
which (apparently) it first arises in the mind, into a surface
structure before it can be 'phonetically interpreted', that is,
expressed in vocal sounds.

To my mind the 'deep structure' on which Chomsky has so
much to say is a phrase which stands for no intelligible mental
operation. The normal man has ideas or thoughts, which
correspond more or less accurately to those things in his
environment which, in the course of his life, he has experienced. He has learnt to give names to the more conspicuous
or, to him, more important features of his world and also to
his own reactions. Since he has learnt these names from the
people among whom he has grown up, he shares the names
with them, and can use them to convey his thoughts to them
and to understand what they say. As for the arrangement of
these words in sentences, the only universal rule is that it must
be such as to make one's meaning understood. For this purpose, those words must be brought together which represent

the ideas which are related to one another in his thoughts. Since very many generations have faced this problem before him, he finds that there have been established a number of grammatical and syntactical conventions which contribute to this result. For instance, words which have to be brought together are linked either by being put next to each other (giving what one might call a rational word-order), or by being given the same endings or inflexions, as in Greek or Latin, or by a combination of both these devices. Chomsky fails to realize that the rules of grammar and syntax laid down in the grammar books are based on the common practice of popular writers, and that the writers themselves, who naturally wish to be understood, have learnt from experience how to express themselves clearly and without ambiguity. Very many people, of course, never learn to do this. If we do in fact, as Chomsky seems to suppose, inherit our grammatical rules, it is surprising how many people learn at an early age to suppress their inherited tendencies.

The popularity of Chomsky's views seems to be due to the fact that they are accepted as the only reasonable alternative to behaviourism — a school of psychology founded in 1919 by J.B. Watson's book *Psychology from the Standpoint of a Behaviorist*. Watson does not regard the brain and nervous system as of much importance for the purpose of explaining thought and the thinking process. He proposes that thought is merely speech, and that speech is essentially a form of muscular or glandular activity. When a man is silently thinking, says Watson, his laryngeal muscles and the muscles of his tongue are active and are 'carrying out as orderly a system of movements as if he were executing a sonata on the piano'. True, we cannot detect any such movements, but this, says Watson, is because our methods of observation are inadequate. This theory seems to reduce man to something little better than an automaton. All religion and philosophy are reduced to a series of imperceptible laryngeal twitchings, no more significant than the creakings of a door. As for the learning process, Watson reduces this to a simple matter of stimulus and response. Rats, for instance, learn their way through mazes by practice, and by 'reinforcement', i.e. they are rewarded (with food) when they take the correct path.

It is as though Chomsky and his followers regarded their linguistic theories as the only escape from the view that human beings learn their language as rats learn their way through mazes; for he stresses that, as soon as we hear a sentence, even though we have never heard this precise sentence before, we immediately understand it because of some inherited 'creative' ability. He seems to suppose that the alternative to his own theory involves the assumption that a man would have to hear every sentence repeated a hundred times, with 'reinforcement' before he could make use of it himself (cf. *Current Issues*, pp.21-22). But in fact Chomskyism is not the only alternative to behaviourism. The process of learning by which a human being becomes a skilled tennis-player is very different from that by which the rat learns to escape from his maze. 'Reinforcement' (in the sense of immediate reward) is not essential, and practice is not the same, for the human can learn a great deal from instruction and imitation. Watson and Chomsky both believe that rational thought is essentially dependent on language and consists in a kind of internal conversation of the soul with itself. But for Watson the conversation is purely muscular, whereas for Chomsky it is more mysterious, and language, as its medium, becomes accordingly mysterious too. It is because he believes that thinking is only talking to oneself that he reduces logic, or correct thinking, to grammar, and says very little about meaning.

In discussing the difference between animal communication and human language, Chomsky refers to the views of Descartes. In the seventeenth century all theorizing on human behaviour was dangerous, and Descartes had to be very careful to draw a clear distinction between man and the 'brutes'. Accordingly, he produced a theory to show that man alone has an eternal spirit, all other animals being mere automata. Here is what he says in a letter to the Marquis of Newcastle which is quoted by Chomsky in translation (*Cartesian Linguistics*, p.5):

> Enfin il n'y a aucune de nos actions extérieures, qui puisse assurer ceux qui les examinent, que notre corps n'est pas seulement une machine qui se remue de soi-même, mais qu'il y a aussi en lui une âme qui a des pensées, excepté les paroles, ou autres signes faits à propos des sujets qui se

présentent, sans se rapporter à aucune passion. (Letter dated 23 November 1646)

(The last phrase was no doubt intended to exclude the cries and songs of beasts and birds). The translation used by Chomsky is so carelessly written that it disguises the very point that Chomsky's argument requires. Descartes here maintains, what he has argued at greater length in the *Discours*, that the soul is the seat of the reason and that the brutes have no reason, since they have no real language. He adds that the resemblance between the 'organs' of animals and men is so great that this might be thought to justify the presumption that animals had some sort of reasoning faculty like men. Against this view he says that, if animals could reason, they must have immortal souls; that however plausible this might be of some animals, it could hardly be true of oysters and sponges; yet if it was true of some it must be true of all. One can only comment that, since the argument for allowing souls to animals rested on the similarity of their 'organs' to those of man, the difficulty of allowing immortal souls to oysters and sponges seems slightly irrelevant. But one can readily understand how Descartes came to argue as he did. If one does not believe in a soul, it is hard to believe in our immortality, for it is all too evident that our bodies are mortal. But it is hard to suppose that an oyster has an immortal soul, and so we have to draw the line somewhere. There is, of course, a great deal more difference between an oyster and any vertebrate than between any vertebrate and man, so that we might—more generously than Descartes—draw the line between the vertebrates and the invertebrates. But the view that language is the hall-mark of the possession of a soul saves us from the distasteful necessity of sharing eternity with the codfish and the monkey.

Descartes is probably not to be taken too seriously on this dangerous topic. At the beginning of the sixth part of the *Discours* he refers, without mentioning names, to the condemnation of Galileo, and tells how the news of this event had led him to refrain from publishing a book which he had ready for the printer, out of deference to the authority of those responsible for the condemnation. What is astonishing is that

Chomsky in the second half of the twentieth century should seek support for his theories from such a source.

(iii) Philosophers
  (a) *Russell*
Bertrand Russell has discussed language in more than one of his books. The passages quoted below, taken from his *Outline of Philosophy,* illustrate his manner of dealing with the subject.

Russell thinks that the study of language must begin with a consideration of three matters:

> First: what words are, regarded as physical occurrences; secondly, what are the circumstances that lead us to use a given word; thirdly, what are the effects of our hearing or seeing a given word. But as regards the second and third of these questions, we shall find ourselves led on from words to sentences and thus confronted with fresh problems, perhaps demanding rather the methods of Gestaltpsychologie.

For single words Russell is satisfied with the 'methods' of the behaviourists (on whom cf. above, p.154). He even regards 'the theory of language as one of the strongest points in favour of behaviourism'. He divides 'ordinary words' into four kinds: spoken, heard, written, and read. He begins with the spoken word, and explains that it consists of a series of movements in the larynx and the mouth, combined with breath. Although he does not mention the meaning he evidently assumes that it is part of the word, for he goes on:

> Two closely similar series of such movements may be instances of the same word, though they may also not be, since two words with different meanings may *sound* alike; but two such series which are not closely similar cannot be instances of the same word.

How close the similarity must be it is hard, he admits, to determine. But, he asks, is it not just as difficult sometimes to know whether a man is running or walking as whether he has said 'dog' or 'dock'? This is a strange comparison, since it is clearly the meaning of the speaker which settles the matter in the one case, but by no means the intention of the competitor in the other. So that it is not quite certain whether he intends us to take account of the meaning in the definition of the spoken word or not. If not, then the identity of a word can be determined only by a delicate sound-recording apparatus; and even this would serve only if we could always infer the spoken word from the heard word, which, as we shall see from a later part of the exposition, is doubtful. And in that case 'pear', 'pair' and 'pare' are all the same word. On the other hand, if the meaning is allowed to count, then the whole question becomes far more complicated than is here suggested.

Having dealt thus with the spoken word, he goes on to discuss the heard word, and says:

> We usually take for granted the relation between a word spoken and a word heard. 'Can you hear what I say?' we ask, and the person addressed says 'yes'. This is of course a delusion, a part of the naive realism of our unreflective outlook on the world. We never hear what is said; we hear something having a complicated causal connection with what is said. There is first the purely physical process of sound-waves from the mouth of the speaker to the ear of the hearer, then a complicated process in the ear and nerves, and then an event in the brain, which is related to our hearing of the sound in a manner to be investigated later, but is at any rate simultaneous with our hearing of the sound. This gives the physical causal connection between the word spoken and the word heard.

We are here asked to regard it as a naive delusion when a man supposes himself to have heard what another man has said. We are asked to believe that it is an important analytical process to split up the hearing of speech into a series of 'physical' phases, sound-waves, nerve currents, events in the brain. And yet, after all, none of these phases, apparently, constitutes the hearing of the word. The 'event in the brain', he says in the passage quoted, 'is related to our hearing of the sound . . . , is at any rate simultaneous with our hearing of the sound'. So that this 'physical causal connection' is distinct from the hearing, and therefore does not help us to understand what it is that we hear, if we do not hear the words.

Can we be expected to believe that this more complicated

account of the matter is any less objectionable than the natural one? What exactly is the 'delusion' involved when we say and believe that we see or hear or feel some event or object in our neighbourhood? Ought we to feel only the feeling, or hear, perhaps, the event in the brain? 'In order that speech may serve its purpose', he says, 'it is not necessary, as it is not possible, that heard and spoken words should be identical, ...' This seems like saying that in order that a man may feel the bite of a flea, it is not necessary that the sensation of the man should be identical with the operation of the insect, or that when one is bitten by an adder one must be careful not to confound the pain with the poison.

It is apparent that Bertrand Russell has failed to distinguish the 'thing' from its 'aspects'. What we call a 'word' is something that can be spoken and heard, written and read, remembered and forgotten, pronounced and mispronounced, understood and misunderstood, inferred, intended, implied, used and misused in countless different ways, and there really is no point in pretending that all these are different kinds of word. It is true that no neat and concise definition is possible for so complex a reality, but in that respect the 'word' does not differ from the 'thought' or the 'thing'. And in biology one gets used to this lack of 'logical' tidiness. The physiologist of course seeks the link that connects the outward and visible reactions with the nervous phenomena in sense organ and brain. But these summary references to sound-waves, 'complicated' processes in ear and nerves, and the 'event in the brain', can scarcely be regarded as a contribution to the physiological analysis.

Russell turns next to what he calls 'the psychological side' of the matter and says that there are two questions to answer: what sort of behaviour is stimulated by hearing a word, and what sort of occasion stimulates us to the behaviour that consists in pronouncing a word? The answer to the first question is:

A child learns to understand words exactly as he learns any other process of bodily association. If you always say 'bottle' when you give a child his bottle, he presently reacts to the word 'bottle', within limits, as he formerly reacted to the bottle. . . . When the association has been established, parents say that the child 'understands' the word 'bottle', or knows what the word 'means'. Of course the word does not have all the effects that the actual bottle has. It does not exert gravitation, it does not nourish, it cannot bump on to the child's head. The effects which are shared by the word and the thing are those which depend upon the law of association or 'conditioned reflexes' or 'learned reactions'.

His account ends with the sentence:

The child becomes excited when he sees the bottle; this is already a conditioned reflex, due to experience that this sight precedes a meal. One further stage in conditioning makes the child grow excited when he hears the word 'bottle'. He is then said to 'understand' the word.

Thus, some undescribed reaction, called 'getting excited', which has previously become linked to the sight of the bottle, may become linked to the sound of the word 'bottle'. It may, of course, equally well, become linked to the sound of the milk being poured into the bottle, or of the bottle being placed on the table, or to any other sound, sight or sensation. In this the sound of the word does not differ from any other stimulus. But why should this be called 'understanding' the word? It may be as much as can be expected of a few-months-old babe. But is this account of the matter supposed to suffice in the case of intelligent adults? It would appear so, for he goes on:

We may say, then, that a person understands a word which he hears if, so far as the law of conditioned reflexes is applicable, the effects of the word are the same as those of what it is said to 'mean'. This of course only applies to words like 'bottle', which denote some concrete object or some class of concrete objects. To understand a word such as 'reciprocity' or 'republicanism' is a more complicated matter, and cannot be considered until we have dealt with sentences.

But why are 'reciprocity' and 'republicanism' more difficult than 'bottle'? Is it because they do not denote a class of concrete objects? Yet if I say to Sarah 'Trust!', she sits still and allows me to place a biscuit on her nose. Does she 'understand' the word? If I say to her 'We are going for a walk', she too becomes excited — to express it rather mildly. But is there any word like 'bottle' in the sentence?

Perhaps the meaning is that the few-months-old babe cannot appreciate the ethical or political implications of these long words, and therefore cannot be said to understand what they mean. But may we then assume that a child of such tender age could have already penetrated to the full significance even of the word 'bottle'? There seems to be still some ambiguity about the word 'meaning'. And how are we to find out precisely where the 'law of conditioned reflexes' is and is not applicable? It is applicable to 'bottle' but not to 'reciprocity'? Would it not be simpler to say that a person understands a word when he knows what it means? For any rational purpose, of course, it would. But when we are trying to talk the 'language' of the behaviourists, we are not allowed to use words like 'know' and 'think', because they imply hidden processes in the mind. And what Russell is, I think, trying to explain is how we may describe in terms of visible behaviour the process of understanding a word. And his answer is this: There are a number of things like bottles, that is to say concrete objects. Each of them has a name. And to understand the name of an object is to react to the name as one would react to the object itself — so far, that is, as the 'law of conditioned reflexes is applicable'. He later illustrates his theory by saying that 'the word "Peter" means a certain person if the associative effects of hearing the word "Peter" are closely similar to those of seeing Peter'.

It is hard to see how any of this can be seriously maintained. First, it is surely a strange theory of 'meaning' according to which the word 'Aristotle' may be said to mean the Greek philosopher who bore that name, only if my reaction to the sound of the word is closely similar to that which would be evoked by the appearance of the philosopher in person; or the word 'tiger' to mean the creature so named only if on hearing it I acted as I should if I met one in the garden. Second, even in the case of simple vertebrates such as fish, it would be most misleading to say that when some noise or sight or smell has become recognized as the signal of a coming event, the reaction to the signal is the same as, or even necessarily resembles, the normal reaction to the event signalled. There may be common components in the two reactions; but usually the signal elicits only a preparatory movement. If you feed fishes with a brush, the approach of the instrument will be recognized as a signal and the fish may move towards it as if it were the actual food, which in fact it very approximately is. But if, when about to feed them, you switch on a light, you will get in the same way some preparatory behaviour at the signal, but it will not be related to the light in the same way as the effective response is related to the food. And so, if the baby's reaction to the bottle is to try to clasp it, the reaction to the name of the bottle can scarcely be the same. The truth is, of course, that the process of learning is more complicated than this formula suggests, and it cannot be summarized by the phrase 'law of conditioned reflexes'.

We now turn to the question of speech and the things which cause us to utter words.

> When a person knows how to speak, the conditioning process proceeds in the opposite direction to that which operates in understanding what others say. The reaction of a person who knows how to speak, when he notices a cat, is naturally to utter the word 'cat'; he may not actually do so, but he will have a reaction leading towards this act, even if, for some reason, the overt act does not take place. It is true that he may utter the word 'cat' because he is 'thinking' about a cat, not actually seeing one. This, however, as we shall see in a moment, is merely one further stage in the process of conditioning. The use of single words, as opposed to sentences, is wholly explicable, so far as I can see, by the principles which apply to animals in mazes.

It should be noted that the word 'thinking' needs the protection of inverted commas, since for a behaviourist this innocent word is suspect. Now what exactly are we to understand by a 'reaction leading towards' an act? Is there an impulse or an inclination? Does this mean that whenever you catch sight of a cat or a dog, you have an urge to exclaim 'Cat!' or 'Dog!', and that if you refrain from doing so there must be some special restraining influence? Is the same true of everything else for which we have learned a name? Must I suppress an impulse to say 'lamppost' or 'pillarbox' or 'bicycle' whenever I encounter one of these in the street? Or is there some other way of explaining why 'the overt act does not take place'? For an observant person who takes an intelligent interest in what goes on in the world, there are numberless things which do not even have a name. The conventional 'things' which form the limited stock-in-trade of philosophical illustration, and the nursery objects on which the child first practises his lessons in talking, may produce the kind of reaction which Russell has in mind. But let anyone try to describe the familiar furniture of his household, and he will discover how many things he sees and handles and uses every day and yet for which he has no ready name nor any need for one.

So far Russell has been discussing only words. Coming now to the problem of sentences, he dismisses, with a touch of humorous banter, the view of 'certain philosophers' that 'the sentence comes first and the single word later'. Here it is worth-while explaining — as Russell does not explain — in what sense such a view has been held, since the proposition that 'the sentence comes first' conveys little until we know what is meant by a sentence.

Now something very like this was, in fact, asserted in 1880 by A.H. Sayce in his *Introduction to the Science of Language,* one of the saner treatises in the immense and arid literature of the subject. He wrote (I, 110):

> The origin of language, then, is to be sought in *gestures, onomatopoeia,* and to a limited extent *interjectional cries.* Like the rope-bridges of the Himalayas or the Andes, they formed the first rude means of communication between man and man . . . . Thus, by imitating the gurgling of water and pointing to the mouth, a man could signify what we express by the sentence, 'I wish to drink', or 'I am thirsty'; . . . In course of time a collection of words would be formed, each of which represented what we now call a sentence.

In short, words were first used in concrete situations for practical purposes, and functioned as statements or questions or commands. But in developed languages these are all held by grammarians to be expressed by sentences, so that, as Sayce says, 'each of these words represented what we now call a sentence'. It is possible to maintain, as against this view, that words were first used in conjunction with a mainly gestural language, and served as signs for things or actions in communications which were principally conveyed by other means. But even this is suggested by Sayce, and he would probably have agreed that purely verbal sentences, unassisted by gesture, would be rare.

Russell indicates the new considerations which have to be explained apropos of sentences in the following passage:

> The first sentences used by children are always repetitions, unchanged, of sentences they have heard used by others. Such cases raise no new principle not involved in the learning of words. What does raise a new principle is the power of putting together known words into a sentence which has never been heard, but which expresses correctly what the infant wishes to say. This involves the power to manipulate form and structure. It does not of course involve the apprehension of form and structure in the abstract, any more than the use of the word 'man' involves apprehension of a universal. But it does involve a causal connection between the form of the stimulus and the form of the reaction. An infant very soon learns to be differently affected by the statement 'cats eat mice' from the way he would be affected by the statement 'mice eat cats'; and not much later he learns to make one of these statements rather than the other. In such a case, the cause (in hearing) or the effect (in speaking) is a whole sentence. It may be that one part of the environment is sufficient to cause one word, while another is sufficient to cause another, but it is only the two parts in their relation that can cause the whole sentence. Thus wherever sentences come in we have a causal relation between two complex facts, namely the fact asserted and the sentence asserting it; the facts as wholes enter into the cause-and-effect relation, which cannot be explained wholly as compounded of relations between their parts.

What is the reader to make of a passage such as this? Does the 'power to manipulate form and structure' mean anything other than the power to discriminate between, say, 'dog' and 'god', or between 'water-tap' and 'tap-water'? What is meant by the 'relation of cause and effect' in this connexion? Is it implied that the spoken sentence 'cats eat mice' causes some specific affection in the child, or that when the child utters such a sentence itself, the word 'cat' is caused by the presence of a cat, the word 'mouse' by that of a mouse, and the whole sentence by a cat and mouse together? What can be meant by 'one part of the environment' and the 'two parts in their relation'? A particular cat with its particular dinner, or cats in general with their particular dinners? What are we to understand by a 'fact as a whole'? Rather than saying that a sentence is 'caused' by the fact which it asserts (which incidentally would leave the greater part of human speech unaccounted for), why should we not take the more normal and intelligible view that a sentence may serve to *convey* the fact which it asserts?

Russell's next paragraph plunges us into further confusion:

> The correct use of relational words, i.e. of sentences, involves what may be correctly termed 'perception of form', i.e. it involves a definite reaction to a stimulus which is a form. Suppose, for example, that a child has learned to say that one thing is 'above' another when this is in fact the case. The stimulus to the use of the word 'above' is a relational feature of the environment, and we may say that this feature is 'perceived' since it produces a definite reaction. It may be said that the relation *above* is not very like the word 'above'. That is true; but the same is true of ordinary physical objects. A stone, according to physicists, is not at all like what we see when we look at it, and yet we may be correctly said to 'perceive' it. This, however, is to anticipate. The definite point which has emerged is that, when a person can use sentences correctly, that is a proof of sensitiveness to formal or relational stimuli.

The reasoning in this passage seems to run as follows:

First statement. We may say that the relational feature represented by the word 'above' is *perceived* because it produces a definite reaction.

Objection. But the relational feature is quite unlike the word used to denote it.

Rejoinder. True, but a stone is quite unlike what we see when we look at it.

Now what is the point of the objection? Why should anybody who finds such a view satisfactory in other respects object to it on the ground that the word does not resemble the relation? How can a word resemble anything except another word? The reply to this queer objection is equally curious. 'A stone is not at all like what we see when we look at it.' Part of the confusion seems to come from an uncertainty whether the word 'above' constitutes the 'perception' or is merely evidence of perception. If it *is* the perception then there is a certain coherence in the argument, which would take the form: The perception of a stone is not like the stone, why should the perception of a relation be like the relation? The behaviourist holds that thoughts are nothing but words uttered inaudibly. Hence the perception of a stone is nothing but the word 'stone'. Unfortunately the reference to the physicists suggests something else. The physicist's idea of a stone, according to Russell, is a system of atoms and electrons, and 'what we see when we look at it' is not atoms and electrons. But neither is it the word 'stone'!

In truth, of course, our ideas do resemble real things. A sane man's idea of his wife and children, his house and his garden, resembles the reality. The fact that we cannot see with our eyes or hear with our ears the molecular or electronic structures which are merely schemes for the interpretation of the behaviour of things no more justifies Russell's view than our inability to distinguish the droplets justifies us in saying that we cannot see the cloud. It is just as legitimate to say that the stone *is* what we see as to say that it is what the physicists say about it. One might as well maintain that what we see with the unaided eye is less real than what we can see with the microscope, that the music we hear is less real than the groove on the gramophone record. But once it has been realized that things have many aspects, far more aspects than any man can ever exhaust, and that a man's idea of the thing is composed of those aspects with which he is acquainted, then these metaphysical difficulties vanish.

(b) *Ayer*

A.J. Ayer's book *Language, Truth and Logic* may bear some

responsibility for the opinion, strongly held today by some professors of linguistics, that all logical thinking depends on the conventions of language, and that accordingly the experts in language are in a position to call the tune.

According to Ayer, science and philosophy are concerned with propositions. Of these there are three kinds: metaphysical or pseudo-propositions, tautologies or *a priori* propositions (also called 'analytical propositions'), and factual or empirical propositions. The first kind, he says, are nonsensical (p.41); the practical test of a nonsensical proposition is the impossibility of deducing from it anything that is verifiable. The second kind (tautologies) 'do not in themselves contain any information about any matter of fact' (p.87). Their validity is 'independent of the nature of the external world' and also 'of the nature of our minds' (p.84). Tautologies, since they are independent of facts, are not verifiable, but, according to Ayer's theory, they are not nonsense. On the contrary, they constitute for him the essential material of philosophy. And because they are independent of facts, 'philosophical analysis is independent of any empirical assumptions' (p.57). The third and last kind of proposition is the empirical proposition or statement of fact. Such statements are verifiable. They are subject to practical test.

Thus, for metaphysical propositions we can devise no test. For the analytical proposition no test is needed, for tautologies cannot be doubted or questioned. Tests are applicable only to the empirical propositions of science and common sense. But such tests can never establish the truth of a proposition with certainty. 'No proposition which has a factual content can be necessary or certain' (p.72). A proposition whose validity depends on experience 'cannot be seen to be necessarily and universally true' (p.75).

Ayer insists that the propositions of philosophy, the tautologies,

> are not factual but linguistic in character — that is, they do not describe the behaviour of physical, or even mental, objects; they express definitions, or the formal consequences of definitions. (p.57)

The philosopher is concerned not with facts, nor with ideas, but with words and their relationships (p.59), with linguistic conventions. He does not invent the rules of language but interprets and elucidates them. He decides, not on their application—for that would involve a reference to empirical and verifiable facts—but on their coherence and compatibility. He shows how one rule may be deduced from another, how this rule is compatible with that. He is, therefore, occupied chiefly with the business of definition, and definition consists in establishing correspondences between verbal formulas.

> Thus in specifying the language to which he intends his definitions to apply, the philosopher is simply describing the conventions from which his definitions are deduced; and the validity of the definitions depends solely on their compatibility with these conventions. (p.70)

How these conventions of language are established and by whom and on what basis is not apparent from Ayer's account. Nor does he explain how rules can be judged to be consistent without reference to some independent criterion. Of course, in constructing an arbitrary language one may prescribe that one symbol or group of symbols shall be held equivalent to another. But nothing can be deduced from such equivalence except on the strength of some independent convention.

Ayer reiterates that self-evident propositions owe their manifest truth to their consistency with linguistic conventions. He instances 'the proposition that a material thing cannot be in two places at once', and says that it is not empirical at all but linguistic. It

> simply records the fact that, as the result of certain verbal conventions, the proposition that two sense-contents occur in the same visual or tactual sense-field is incompatible with the proposition that they belong to the same material thing. And this is indeed a necessary fact. But . . . it is necessary only because we happen to use the relevant words in a particular way. There is no logical reason why we should not so alter our definitions that the sentence 'A thing cannot be in two places at once' comes to express a self-contradiction instead of a necessary truth. (p.58)

Why we 'happen to use' words in this way might be supposed to be a historical question. But that implies the possibility of discovering the reasons for the linguistic convention, and this would be a matter of fact and so undermine the independence of the analytic proposition. Ayer's view seems to be that the conventions are man-made but must be perfectly arbitrary. According to him we do not assert that one thing cannot be in two places at the same time because of any experience we or our ancestors have had. We make the assertion because we like to have our language arranged that way. We might just as well have decided to say that no thing can be in less than three or more than five places at one time. If we—that is to say, if Adam and Eve—had so decided then this would have become a self-evident proposition, an analytic truth, a tautology. It is just a matter of luck that our language should seem to be justified by vulgar experience. The reader may think the reference to Adam and Eve a little frivolous. But since all known languages seem to have adopted the same convention, this convention must date from the very beginnings of language. What are usually understood as linguistic conventions differ considerably in different languages. The universal adoption of the conventions which underlie these 'self-evident' truths is surely in need of some explanation.

Ayer argues that tautologies are *a priori* propositions—i.e. they are independent of experience—because they are universally and necessarily true, and experience could at best establish their truth in particular instances.

> No general proposition whose validity is subject to the test of actual experience can ever be logically certain. No matter how often it is verified in practice, there still remains the possibility that it will be confuted on some future occasion. The fact that a law has been substantiated in $n-1$ cases affords no logical guarantee that it will be substantiated in the nth case also, no matter how large we take n to be. (p.72)

One cannot help wondering how he recognizes an *a priori* proposition when he meets it. It is clear from the reference to 'logical' certainty that he includes the truths of logic among the tautologies, the *a priori* propositions which are necessarily true. He also puts mathematical propositions into this class, and to substantiate his assertion that 'the truths of formal logic and pure mathematics are necessarily true' he adopts the method of examining cases 'in which they might seem to be confuted'. If, he says, on counting what he had taken to be five pairs of objects, he found only nine, he would not conclude that the mathematical proposition '2 × 5 = 10' had been confuted (p.75). In other words, in the case of a particular failure, we resort to any hypothesis rather than abandon the multiplication tables. That is true; but it does not distinguish mathematical propositions from other admittedly empirical generalizations. If I am told that a man has been seen to leap off the Monument, soar into the air over the river, and alight upon a pinnacle of the Tower Bridge, I shall adopt any hypothesis rather than throw over the law of gravitation. Our faith in gravitation may not be quite so strong as our faith in the multiplication tables, but then our experience has been vitiated by apparent exceptions; and it is not quite impossible to doubt the universal validity of the fundamental operations of arithmetic. The difference is one of degree.

In Ayer's view it is the task of philosophy to provide definitions; in particular, to define the various possible 'transformations' which can be carried out on words and sentences.

The attempt to arrive at truth through the manipulation of words is a centuries-old philosophers' dream. It is partly based on the notion that language is, or could be made to be, a symbolic *system*, analogous to mathematics, which enables the user to infer the nature of reality from a proper manipulation of the symbols. I have endeavoured to show, in Chapter 12, that this is an illusion. No inferences drawn from an arbitrary system of symbols can have any significance except in relation to some other correlated system. The only correlated system that could be claimed for language would be the whole system of nature; and for such a purpose the trivial resources of language, even if all the contrivances of grammar and syntax of all the languages in the world were combined and all their vocabularies added together, would be utterly inadequate. If, therefore, the philosopher — as Ayer assures us — is really restricted to propositions about language, to definitions and inferences from definitions, and is debarred from making any use of experimental facts, then it is not possible that he should make any contribution to knowledge. Aristotle's belief that the rules of logic, if one could only fix them correctly, would enable one to pass infallibly from verbal inferences to material consequences, rests, of course, like other magical beliefs, on the observation of real correlations. It is only the generalization that is at fault. If there were no correlation at all between verbal sequences and reality, then language would be less significant than the song of the cicada. But what correlation there is has been laboriously put there by countless generations of experimenters. And inferences from the conventional structure of language to the natural structure of our environment are no more reliable than other forms of proverbial wisdom.

Conclusion

Language, as we know it, consists in communication by means of arbitrary signs. The use of language is a peculiarly human accomplishment, and for those who wish to believe in a fundamental difference between man and other animals, the existence of language has provided comfort and reassurance. Those who believe in the continuity of our species with a species of higher ape are faced with the problem of explaining how language could possibly have developed in a creature not possessing this faculty, without recourse to psychological principles which cannot be shown to apply to the higher apes. This I have endeavoured to do.

One of the most important factors was the aggregation of men into social groups. In such groups the individual must adapt his behaviour as much to that of his companions as to the rest of his environment. With chimpanzees and, presumably, with primitive man, thinking was mainly concerned with concrete things, material objects and palpable physical processes, including the animal's own actions. But with social habits, the development of tools, co-operation in hunting, agriculture, etc., the need for communication led to the development of special techniques. Drawing, modelling, pantomime, gesture, vocal imitations would all have been made use of where they lent themselves to the immediate purpose. Pantomime was very expressive, but unsuitable for rapid communication. Drawing and modelling were inconvenient. But for a long time every possible means must have been employed, each supplementing the other. Gradually the signs used became conventionalized — i.e. lost some of their primitive intelligibility to all except to those who were making constant use of them. The language of the deaf and dumb as practised today is quite meaningless to the ordinary spectator; it is completely conventionalized. But with this loss of universal intelligibility goes a great increase in efficiency as a means of communication between the initiated. In the same way picture-writing became conventionalized and gained in efficiency while it ceased to be understood by all except the scribes. As soon as it became clear that self-explanatory signs were unnecessary, as soon as it was seen that quite arbitrary conventionalized gestures and signs could be understood by those who had learned to use them, and were much more convenient and concise, then conventional sounds began to be used also; and it was discovered that they had great advantages over all other forms of communication. Gesture-language survived as a substitute or auxiliary method for special purposes, and pantomime survives today in various forms of religious ritual. Models were used for magical and religious purposes, and much later on for scientific ones. It is obvious also that all the divers forms of primitive communication gave rise to special forms of what we now call 'art'. Sculpture, painting and the drama are the most conspicuous. The development of poetry — that is, of formalized language — can be largely attributed to the fact that formalized utterances are relatively easy to memorize.

If we reject theories involving magical intervention, there is no reasonable alternative to the view that language was invented. This view has been put forward often, and as often dismissed on the grounds of Rousseau's paradox — that language could not have been invented without the existence of a language. The answer to the paradox is now, I hope, clear. Spoken language is not, and has never been, the sole means of communication between men. Even today, the multiplicity of languages necessitates the use of gestures, pictures and other expedients for communication between people of different tongues. These were in use before spoken languages existed. The first forms of communication were self-explanatory. Arbitrary systems — and this includes all the known spoken languages — were invented later. The fact that they are arbitrary is sufficient evidence that they were invented. Their invention would not have been possible without the earlier existence of other means of communication. Like other inventions, language is a tool, the essential feature of which is that arbitrary symbols — words, phrases and sentences — are used to convey ideas. In any language there are conventional ways of combining words in order to express the relations between ideas. These conventions are codified by the grammarians, and the conventions obtaining in different languages are studied and compared by linguists. The fact that there are similarities in the conventions of unrelated languages can be readily explained by the common purpose for which languages were invented, the common features of human physiology, and the common elements in the human environment.

Unfortunately, there is no systematic relationship between ideas and the words which are used to express them. It has too often been supposed that the rules devised by grammarians somehow reflect the rules of clear thinking, and even that a perfect language could be created, which would make misunderstandings impossible. These are illusions. There is only one way of ensuring that an idea has been communicated, and that is to persist, if necessary with the aid of gesture and illustration, until the listener's response shows that the message has been received. No rules can ever be contrived to obviate this necessity. On the other hand, words may be strung together in accordance with the grammarians' rules, and yet express mistaken ideas, or no ideas at all. It is this insecure connexion between words and ideas which bedevils all reasoning that is not closely related to practical experience. It is impossible to construct a grammar without reference to meaning; and the ideas which constitute the meaning of any discourse must refer to the world which we know through our senses, or they are without interest. The rules of logic must likewise be related to our experience of the real world. To equate the rules of logic with the conventions of grammar leads only to futility.

Appendix: The Bowdon Experiments

The experiments were conducted as follows. A number of people, chiefly young boys, but including one girl and two adults, were grouped in pairs, one of whom acted as 'agent' and the other as 'respondent'. Each group of two would operate separately. The agent would receive a piece of paper on which a word was written. He was asked to convey its meaning to his companion, using any means he chose except speaking or writing. In the following record the 91 words employed are set down in the left-hand column. Against these on the right are indicated briefly the signs which were used. Each person is represented by a number. A full account of the experiments would include the interpretation suggested by the respondent. Where I have made no reference to the interpretation it is to be taken that the correct answer was given, though not necessarily at once. I have recorded the wrong interpretations only where they seemed of particular interest.

BOWDON EXPERIMENTS

1. MOUNTAIN	Air-picture. Action of climbing, wiping sweat. 1. Describes outline of hill on picture. 2. Air-picture. 4. (Misunderstood as 'zig-zag'· and 'electricity'.)
2. SORROW	Weeps. 4. Weeps in handkerchief. 12. Looks at watch and knocks finger against it and begins to sob. Puts finger in fire and sobs. 19. (Appears to confound 'sorrow' with 'pain'.)
3. CABHORSE	Crawls along floor pulling chair behind him. 4. Drives and runs, but latter in human position. Trots with bowed head, imitates action of horse with four fingers. 2.
4. WATER	Swimming and drinking action. 1. Wets finger and puts to palm of hand. 2. Drinks from imaginary cup. 10. Movement with newspaper along ground. (Understood as 'shrimping'). 12. Acts as if in water bathing, splashing movement with hand. 25. Breast

stroke. Horizontal movement with hand to indicate 'surface'. Points to sky and indicates falling rain. Points to rain-drops on window. 16.

5. BARREL — Draws shape in air. Action of rolling it. Points to small tin. Rolls this along ground. 1. Imitates filling, tipping and rolling with chair. 4.

6. JAM — Scoops it out, spreads and eats. Uses paper-knife and book. 1. Opens tobacco-tin, scoops out and spreads. 2. Takes from tin, spreads on piece of paper and eats. 4.

7. COAL — Shovels it on fire. 3. Action of breaking and shovelling, picking up pieces and putting on fire. 6. Action of working with pick in mine. 7.

8. FATHER — Points to self, then raises hand to signify 'big'. 3. Points to man in picture and then to self. 5. Pretends to put child over knee and spank it. 6. Nurses cushion. 20.

9. SHIP — Air-picture. 3. Pretends to get into sailing ship and holds tiller, pulls ropes, etc., action of rowing. 5. Air-picture of rolling sea and tossing vessel. 6. Sits on chair and rows. 7.

10. GRASS — Points to green on carpet and makes noise like a donkey. 3. Action with imaginary mowing machine, throwing away grass. Action with imaginary scythe. 5. Represents blades of grass with upturned fingers on ground. Air-picture near ground, points to green patch on carpet. 6. Points to green shelf and then sweeps hand over carpet. Kneels and pretends to chew grass. 10. Points to grass in picture. Passes hand over ground. 12. Pushes chair as mowing machine, picks out grass and holds it up, points to green book, takes off coat, goes on mowing, throws away grass, 20.

11. MUSIC — Action of piano-playing, violin and drum. 3. Pretends to perform on piano, violin, jew's harp and mouth-organ. 5. (Understood as 'instrument', 'playing', etc.)

12. RIVER — Indicates course on ground; shows picture postcard. 3. Pretends to fish with line.

	Swimming action. Makes signs on ground. 5. Rapid sweep of hand, air-picture, zig-zag motion. 6. Makes paper boat and carries it through air as if sailing. 7. Pretends to dig narrow trench and pour water in from a can. 10.
13. FIRE	Points to gas-stove. Imaginary shovelling. Warms his hands. 8. Points to grate. 14. Points to gas-stove. Puts books together on ground as if making a fire. 19.
14. BICYCLE	Movement with one leg and two hands. Draws picture of wheels on ground. 8. Sits on chair and pretends to work pedals. 20.
15. BATTLE	Pretends to fire gun, pistol. Fisticuffs. Makes passes with imaginary sword. Makes drawing of sword on ground. 8. Blows whistle, makes signal for the advance and lies down, then charges. 20.
16. WINTER	Turns up coat collar, draws near fire. Puts on imaginary gloves. 8. Throws scraps of paper in air. 20.
17. BUTTERFLY	Makes wings with two hands and flaps them in the air. 10. Pretends to catch one in his fingers and put it in a tin. 14.
18. PLOUGH	Guides imaginary plough. Picture on the ground. Clicks to imaginary horse. 8. Harnesses horses, walks behind plough, makes movement with hand to indicate ground, turns up furrow with hand, clicks. 20.
19. ARROW	Action of drawing bow and taking arrow from quiver. 8. Pulls imaginary bow, shoots arrow and goes to fetch arrow from wall and shoots again. 13.
20. RAIN	Puts up imaginary umbrella and walks holding it. Takes off coat and holds it before fire. 13. Motion with hand to indicate falling rain. Horizontal movement with hand to indicate water. Taps table with one finger. Pulls coat over head. Repeated movement of hand downward with fingers extended. 24. Turns up coat collar and indicates falling rain with one hand. 27. Turns up coat collar, carries

	umbrella and walks quickly. Puts on goloshes. 8. Puts on overcoat, draws it over his head, and runs about. Holds chair over his head. 11.
21. HUMBLE	Kneels down, bows head, puts hands together and shakes them. 13.
22. WORM	Makes wriggling line with forefinger in air; same on ground. (Understood as blind man reading Braille). 8. Wriggles finger in air. 16. First indicates length, then wriggles with finger on floor. 3. Simulates worm with his whole body, rolling and squirming. 7.
23. BELL	Shows watch set at 9 and rings imaginary bell. Imitates playing of chimes on tubular bells. 3. Pulls imaginary bell-rope. 5. Pulls imaginary bell by fire-place. 7.
24. CAMERA	Arranges imaginary sitter, pulls out imaginary camera and takes picture. 5. Pretends to pull camera from pocket, extend it and look into finder. 3. Takes photo with imaginary camera, presses release and winds film. 7.
25. STREET	Shows picture postcard. 3. Walks, greets friends. Draws imaginary plan on ground. 5. Sweeping gestures with hands in direction of neighbouring streets. Pretends to drive car. Impersonates policeman on traffic duty. 6.
26. COLOUR	Points to books of different colours. Represents artist painting. Points to different colours on carpet. In imitating action of painting uses book for paint-box and newspaper for canvas. 4. Points to different coloured objects. 34.
27. SHOP	Wraps imaginary parcel, hands over counter. Takes down imaginary box from shelf. Pretends to purchase a book. 6.
28. HATCHET	Pretends to cut down brushwood, collect fuel. Beckons for men to help carry log. Chops up small pieces on ground pretending to hold them upright with one hand. 8. Puts chair in middle of room and chops at it. 13.
29. SPADE	Pretends to dig. 10. Shovels and digs. Air-picture. 12.

30. DEATH	Flings up his arms and falls and then lies still. 10. Strangles himself and falls to ground. Stabs himself. 11.
31. HUT	Constructs one out of newspaper. It does not work so he uses books instead. 10. Places two chairs against ledge of desk and crawls beneath. 11. Points to four walls of room, ceiling and floor. (Understood as 'cube' and 'wood'). Sweeping movement of hand in all directions. (Understood as 'room'). Points again to walls, fire and window. 19.
32. SWORD	Beckons respondent and draws picture on ground. Wields imaginary sword. Takes a walking-stick and stabs himself. 10. Fights imaginary duel with ruler. Draws imaginary sword from scabbard. 11. Fences with imaginary rapier. 19.
33. RHINOCEROS	Walks on all fours, rubs head against wall, walks backward. 11. Air-picture. Points to picture of trees. Points to top of his head, butts and points behind him. Waves finger over picture of trees (to express many trees or forest?) Picture on ground. 10.
34. SLEEP	Places two hands palm to palm under left cheek, lies on ground. 12. Lies down and shuts eyes. 13. Leans back in chair and snores. 24.
35. FOREST	Upward motion of both hands. Draws picture on wall. Points to trees in picture, counts rapidly on fingers. 12. Pretends to cut down undergrowth with ruler and repeats motion as if with axe or billhook. 13. Drawing. 22.
36. SHIELD	Holds imaginary shield on arm. Air-picture. Holds up newspaper. 12. Takes newspaper and ruler as shield and sword. 13. Holds arm in front of face, cowers behind bent arm, hides behind chair. (Understood as meaning the action 'to shield'). Drawing. 22.
37. LIFE	Points to book and then to himself and jumps. Points to picture, shakes his head and then points to himself. 12. Pretends to kill himself with knife and falls down, then jumps up and waves arms. (Understood first as 'dead'. He

waited motionless on the floor to hear this interpretation before he rose.) 15. Lies on back with eyes closed as if stunned, then looks up in a dazed way as if to show that he is not dead. 18. Broad grin. Wipes his eyes with handkerchief (depicting joy and sorrow?), scratches his head, nurses imaginary baby, using handkerchief as baby, whimpers, lies down on his back. Drawing. 22.

38. SPRING — Shivers, then motion with fingers, 12. Picture. 17.

39. HORSE — All fours, motion with hands over back (to indicate rider). (Understood as 'duck'). 12.

40. SEA — Fishes with imaginary line. Movement of hands to indicate level of sea. Sits on chairs and makes motion of rowing. Draws picture on ground. 14. (Understood as 'boat' and 'fish'). Imaginary picture with finger of sailing ship with sea all round much emphasized. (Understood as 'boat' and 'water'). Jumps off chair into boat, loosens sail and takes tiller in hand, again indicating sea with sweeping gesture. Digs in sand, fetches water in imaginary bucket. (Understood as 'water'). Runs into sea and starts swimming. (Understood as 'fish'). Breast stroke, indicating sea-level as before. Pretends to duck his head. 14.

41. BLOOD — Pinches himself and draws blood. 15. Sharpens pencil, misses the pencil and pretends to cut himself, sucks finger, points to imaginary drop of blood on ground. 18. Points to inside of lip, also a red tablecloth. Draws knife and pretends to cut himself. 19.

42. ANGER — Looks ferocious, hits out and kicks. 14. Clenches fists and stamps his feet, beats fist into palm of hand. (Understood as 'fighting', 'hammering', 'hitting'). 23. Beckons respondent, makes him hold his hand and pretends to cane him. (Understood as 'cane'). Pushes him back into his chair. (Understood as 'disgrace'). Makes him get down on all fours and pretends to thrash him. (Understood as 'hiding', 'cruelty' and 'beating'). 28.

43. NOTHING	Puts five articles together on table and then removes them, indicating the empty space. (Understood as 'clearance'). Empties match-box and shows it. (Understood as 'empty'). Empties ashtray. (Understood as 'clean'). 15. Takes off shoe, points inside it, waves hands and shrugs his shoulders. 18. Shrugs shoulders with outstretched hands. 25. Looks into purse and puts on expression of dismay. 27.
44. SPIDER	Picture. 15. Creeps his hand along floor. (Understood as 'beetle', 'elephant', 'mouse', 'chicken'). Climbs up chair with his hand, up wall, catches and eats imaginary fly, wraps web around fly. 18. Points to corner of room and makes movement to suggest spider falling on strand of web and then runs fingers along ground. 19.
45 AUTUMN	Picture. Points to trees and taps paper with finger. 15. Points to tree in picture. Indicates falling leaves by downward, sweeping motion of hand. 19.
46. BED	Shows imaginary bed to respondent and lies on ground. 16.
47. FISH	Swimming. Indicates water level above his head. Draws fish on table. Waggles hand in air, pretends to eat picture he has drawn. 16. Lies on stomach and swims. Pretends to be fishing. Holds imaginary fish before fire and then eats. 18. Indicates level of water by undulating hand. Lies on stomach, moves elbows as fins, raises both feet together for tail. 19.
48. TREE	Points to wooden table, air-pictures of trunk and branches, picture on table. 16.
49. HAMMER	Action with both hands. (Understood as 'bell'). Picture on table. 16.
50. HAND	Picture on table. (Understood as 'rope'). 16.
51. SCISSORS	Action of opening and shutting hand and thumb. Picture. 16.
52. WIND	Rapid sweeping movements with hand indicating rushing of wind. Blows with mouth and repeats movement of hands. 19. Blows with mouth. 23.

53. ELEPHANT	Moves ruler rapidly through air, brings it to his own chest and pretends to be wounded. Shows point and feather of imaginary arrow with finger. (Understood as 'arrow'). 21. Picture on ground, indicates trunk and tusks from his own face. 21.
54. WICKED	Ferocious expression, stabs me with ruler, steals papers from desk. Indicates dock or cell by tracing walls with his hands. 21.
55. SUN	Points to light and indicates motion of sun. 21. Looks up and blinks, shields his eyes, points to electric light. 27. Points up and holds head as if to protect from sun. 24.
56. WORLD	Points in all directions and indicates a round or sphere. 21.
57. CROCODILE	On all fours, using arms to simulate opening jaws. Points to foot (to suggest leather?) Uses sign for sun to indicate hot country. Tries to suggest hardness of skin. 24.
58. HIGH	Stretches up with hand, indicates level of head, stretches up hand and jumps. Stands on tiptoe with upstretched hand. 24. Puts book on ground and then on shelf and shading his eyes and looks upward and says 'Phew!'. 29. Pretends to throw something into the air, shades his eyes and looks up. 34.
59. MEAT	Carves and eats, points to his own skin, points downstairs (i.e. to dining-room and kitchen). Draws plate on table. Munches. Cuts imaginary piece off cheek. 24. Carves vigorously. 27. Carves, sharpens imaginary knife. Draws leg of mutton on floor. Works jaws with his hands (to indicate toughness?). 34.
60. SHUT	Opens and shuts door. 25.
61. MANY	Sweeping and pointing movements, points to all the books in the bookcases. Stretches arms in opposite directions. 25. Opens and closes fingers rapidly and persistently. Points to many imaginary objects. Points first to one book then to all of them. Indicates one cardboard target and then all of them. 36.
62. EGG	Air-picture. Pretends to open and eat, holding the imaginary egg in left hand. Air-

	picture of egg in egg-cup. Lifts up chicken off her eggs, counts them, goes to another roost and repeats the movements. 27.
63. OPEN	Opens book. (Understood as 'book'). Opens tobacco jar, and then opens door with a special effort. 27.
64. GOOD	Corrects imaginary exercise, claps hands, holds sheet of paper in hand to represent exercise. Pretends to eat something, smiles with pleasure. 27. Pretends to eat, rubs stomach and smiles. 34.
65. GO	Pretends to get on his mark for a race. Points to the starter. Drops handkerchief. 27. Runs round room. 28.
66. LOVE	Sits beside respondent, kisses him, puts imaginary ring on his finger. 27.
67. MINE (i.e. 'my own')	Pretends to attack respondent and takes from him a pen which he had previously put into his pocket. Points at it and at himself. Shows his handkerchief and points at himself, then touches respondent's spectacles and points at respondent. 28.
68. RUN	Runs about room. Puts his pen in respondent's pocket, turns latter round and pretends to run after him. 28.
69. DARK	Gropes about with eyes shut. (Understood as 'blind'). Turns on light and then walks about normally with eyes open. 28. Gropes about, feeling her way, turns the light away and gropes. Looks through keyhole, rests face on folded hands as if to sleep. 35.
70. FLY	Runs about flapping hands like bird. 28. Movement of arms like bird. 35.
71. HOT	Puts hand near fire and pretends to find it hot, snaps fingers as if burnt, wipes forehead, eases his collar. 28.
72. WET	Puts on hat and coat, takes umbrella, turns up collar, puts up umbrella (imaginary), walks about, brushes rain from coat, pretends to take off boots. Umbrella is represented by stick. Makes hissing noise to represent sound of rain. Pretends to wash himself, looks round for towel. Pretends to push up window, puts

up hand, feels rain, takes stick again and puts it up as umbrella. Stands on chair and pretends to dive into water, climbs out, rubs hair and body. 29.

73. SEE

Goes about peering at things, shades his eyes. 29. Shuts his eyes and then opens them. (Understood as 'blind', 'blink', and 'open'). Gazes all round. 34.

74. LONG

Pretends to throw stone or ball. Shades his eyes, measures with his feet, then with a ruler. (Understood as 'length'). 29.

75. TAKE

Takes boots and then puts them back, takes various things and then restores them to their places, takes chair twice round the room and then puts it back in its place. (Understood as 'carry', 'fetch', 'bring', 'give').

76. EMPTY

Takes off shoe and looks inside, opens empty tin and shows it. 34.

77. SAND

Digging, sweeping movement with hand; makes sand castle, pats sides, scoops up imaginary sand in hand, draws line and begins to dig. 34.

78. WISH

Points to letter and counts five on his fingers. Points to money, picture. 34.

79. MOVE

Tries to move bookcase. Moves chair along ground. Shifts books from one shelf to another. 34.

80. HEAR

Puts hand to ear and listens. (Understood as 'deaf'). Beats imaginary drum and listens with hand to ear. 34.

81. HAPPY

Sits and then jumps gleefully. Laughs. (Understood as 'ride', 'jolt'). Dances, waltzes. 35.

82. BAD

Shakes finger at respondent, pretends to hear his lessons, shakes head, points to her forehead and then at respondent. 35.

83. HOUSE

Makes imaginary tiny walls on ground with hands as if of mud, indicates doors and windows with fingers. 35.

84. AIR

Puts hands over respondent's mouth and holds his nose. 36.

85. BLIND

Shuts eyes, puts on hat and walks with stick. 36.

86. NEVER   Indicates to respondent that he must turn out the light, then stops him. Pretends to be boy smoking and then assumes airs of a superior person who never does such a thing. 36.

87. BABY   Indicates a length of two feet and then himself. (Understood as 'measure', 'yourself', 'tiny', 'length', 'dress', 'bone', 'cotton'). Points to respondent and then to himself and again indicates length of baby. (Understood as 'together'). 25.

88. WATERPIPE Wets finger and points to tobacco pipe. 2. (This depends on double meaning of a *word* and was therefore inadmissible).

89. KNIFE   Points to one. 2. Sharpens imaginary pencil with two fingers.

90. TABLE CLOTH Points to it. (Understood as 'white' because he happened to point to white part of cloth.) 2. Spreads newspaper on upturned chair, (Understood as 'butler', 'waiter', 'tea', 'table', 'cloth'). 4.

91. DESERT   Makes sign for sand. 25.

Bibliography

AVEBURY, LORD (J. LUBBOCK) *Marriage, Totemism and Religion*, London, 1911.

AYER, A.J. *Language, Truth and Logic*, 2nd. edn., London, 1946.

BARNETT, H.G. *Innovation. The Basis of Cultural Change*, N.Y., 1953.

BARTON, G.A. *The Origin and Development of Babylonian Writing* (Beiträge zur Assyriologie und semitischen Sprachwissenschaft, Bd. 9, Leipzig, 1913).

BUDGE, E.A.W. *Easy Lessons in Hieroglyphics*, 4th edn., London, 1922.

The Book of the Dead, London, 1928, 2nd edn.

Egyptian Magic, London, no date.

CHILDE, V.G. *Magic, Craftsmanship and Science*, Liverpool, 1949.

CHOMSKY, N. *Cartesian Linguistics*, N.Y. and London, 1966.

Language and Mind, N.Y., 1968.

Current Issues in Linguistic Theory, Paris and the Hague, 1969.

CLARKE, G. AND PIGGOTT, S. *Prehistoric Societies*, London, 1965.

CONDILLAC *Essai sur l'origine des connaissances humaines* (1746). Pt. 2 is entitled 'De l'origine et du progrès du langage'. Printed in *Oeuvres*, Paris, 1798, vol. 1, pp 257ff.

La Logique, ou les premiers développemens de l'art de penser, in *Oeuvres*, as above, vol. 22.

DESCARTES *Principes de la philosophie*, in *Oeuvres et lettres*, in one vol., ed. A. Bridoux, Paris, 1952 (Bibl. de la Pléiade no. 40).

DIAMOND, A.S. *The History and Origin of Language*, London, 1959.

ENGLEFIELD, F.R.H. 'Linguistics: Science or Pseudo-Science?', *Trivium*, 9 (1974), 1-18.

'The Origin, Functions and Development of Poetry', *Trivium*, 10 (1975), 62-73.

FLEMING, JOYCE 'The State of the Apes', *Psychology Today*, 1, (1975) 16-25.

FRAENKEL, G.S. AND GUNN, D.L. *The Orientation of Animals*, Oxford, 1940.

FRAZER, J.G. *Taboo and the Perils of the Soul*, London 1911 (Part 2 of *The Golden Bough*).

Spirits of the Corn and of the Wild, 2 vols., London, 1919 (Part 5 of *The Golden Bough*).

GALTON, F. *Inquiries into Human Faculty*, London, 1883.

GARDNER, BEATRICE AND ALLEN 'Two-Way Communication with an Infant Chimpanzee' *Behaviour of Nonhuman Primates*, ed. A.M. Schrier and F. Stollnitz, N.Y. and London, vol. 4 (1971), 117-184.

HADDON, A.C. *Magic and Fetishism*, London, 1906.

HARRISON, JANE *Ancient Art and Ritual* (Home University Library edn.).

HEGEL, G.W.F. *Phänomenologie des Geistes*, ed. G. Lasson, Leipzig, 1907.

HERDER, J.G. VON *Über den Ursprung der Sprache*, 1772.

HEWES, G.W. *Language Origins: A Bibliography*, Dept. of Anthropology, Univ. of Colorado, Boulder, 1971 (A second, revised edn. has recently been published in two vols., The Hague, 1975).

HUMBOLDT, W. VON *Sprachstudien* = *Abhandlung über das vergleichende Sprachstudium:* in *Die sprachphilosophischen Werke W. von Humboldts*, Berlin, 1883.

JAENSCH, E.R. *Eidetic Imagery*, Engl. trans., London, 1930.

JAMES, W. *The Principles of Psychology*, London, 1901.

JENNINGS, H.S. *Behaviour of the Lower Organisms*, N.Y., 1906.

JESPERSEN, O. *Language, its Nature, Development and Origin*, London, 1947.

The Philosophy of Grammar, London, 1924.

JOHNSTON, H.H. *George Grenfell and the Congo*, 2 vols., London, 1908.

JOWETT see Plato.

KÖHLER, W. *Intelligenzprüfungen an Menschenaffen*, 2nd edn., Berlin, 1921. (Eng. trans. in Pelican Books, 1957).

LANE, E.T. *The Arabian Nights Entertainments*, London, 1928.

The Manners and Customs of the Modern Egyptians, London (Everyman edn.), 1908.

LANGER, SUZANNE K. *Introduction to Symbolic Logic*, 2nd edn., N.Y., Dover Publications, 1953.

LENNEBERG, E. *Biological Foundations of Language*, M.I.T., 1967.

LIEBERMAN, P. *The Speech of Primates*, The Hague, 1972.

LINDEN, E. *Apes, Men and Language*, N.Y., 1975. (Pelican, 1976).

LYONS, J. *Introduction to Theoretical Linguistics*, C.U.P., 1968.

MACCURDY, G.G. *Human Origins*, 2 vols., N.Y. and London, 1924.

MACH, E. *Erkenntnis und Irrtum*, Leipzig, 5th edn., 1926. Eng. trans. *Knowledge and Error*, Dordrecht, 1976.

MALLERY, G. *On the Pictographs of the American Indians*, Washington Govt. Print. Office, 1886.

Sign Language among the North American Indians, Washington (Smithsonian Institute, 1881).

MASPERO, G. *Histoire ancienne des peuples de l'orient*, 4th edn., Paris, 1886.

MONBODDO, LORD (J. BURNET) *The Origin and Progress of Language*, 2nd edn., vol. 1, 1774.

MÜLLER, F. MAX *Lectures on the Science of Language*, 2 vols., London, 1882.

OGDEN, C.K. AND RICHARDS, I.A. *The Meaning of Meaning*, London, 1923.

PAGET, R. *Human Speech*, London, 1930.
'The Origins of Language', *Cahiers d'Histoire Mondiale*, 1 (1953), 399-414.

PARRY, J. *The Psychology of Human Communication*, U.L.P., 1967.

PAVLOV, I.P. *Conditioned Reflexes*, Engl. trans. G.V. Anrep, Oxford, 1927.

PLATO Jowett's *Dialogues of Plato*, 3rd edn., 5 vols., Oxford, 1892.

RENSCH, B. 'Gedächtnis, Abstraktion und Generalisation bei Tieren', *Arbeitsgemeinschaft für Forschung des Landes Nordrhein-Westfalen*, Hft. 114 (1962).

REVESZ, G. *Ursprung und Vorgeschichte der Sprache*, Bern, 1946.

RIGNANO, E. *Psychologie du Raisonnement*, Paris, 1920.

ROTH, H. LING *The Natives of Sarawak and British North Borneo*, 2 vols., London, 1896.

ROUSSEAU, J.J. *Discours sur l'origine de l'inégalité parmi les hommes*, Amsterdam, 1755.

RUSSELL, B. *History of Western Philosophy*, London, 1948.
Outline of Philosophy (Unwin Books), London, 1970.

SAUSSURE, F. *Cours de linguistique générale*, Paris, 1916 (reprinted 1931).

SCHLEGEL, F. *Über die Sprache und Weisheit der Indier*, Heidelberg, 1808.

SCHOOLCRAFT, H.R. See Mallery.

SEIDEL, A. *Chinesische Grammatik*, Heidelberg, 1901.
Suahili Konversations-Grammatik, Heidelberg, 1900.

SHERRINGTON, C.S. *The Integrative Action of the Nervous System*, CUP, 1947.

SMITH, F. AND MILLER, G. (EDITORS) *The Genesis of Language*, Cambridge (Mass.), 1966.

SPENCE, K.W. 'Experimental Studies of Learning and the Higher Mental Processes in Infra-human Primates', *Psychological Bulletin*, vol. 34 (1937).

STEWART, DUGALD *Elements of the Philosophy of the Human Mind*, London, 1814.

SWADESH, M. *The Origin and Diversification of Language*, London, 1972.

THORNDIKE, E.L. *Animal Intelligence*, N.Y., 1911.

TINBERGEN, N. *Social Behaviour in Animals*, London, 1965.

TYLOR, E.B. *The Early History of Mankind*, London, 1865.
Anthropology, London, 1881.

VENN, J. *The Principles of Empirical or Inductive Logic*, 2nd edn., London, 1907.

VYGOTSKY, L.S. *Thought and Language*, ed. and trans. by E. Haufmann and G. Vakar, Cambridge (Mass.), 1939 (republished 1962).

WARBURTON, W. *The Divine Legation of Moses*, vol. 3 (Bk. 4), London, 1765.

WATSON, J.B. *Psychology from the Standpoint of a Behaviorist*, 2nd edn., Philadelphia and London, 1924.

WITTGENSTEIN, L. *Tractatus Logico-philosophicus*, ed. B. Russell, London, 1922.

WUNDT, W. *Völkerpsychologie*, 10 vols., Stuttgart, 1917-22.

Index